The Taizé

MW00710434

❧

LISTENING WITH THE HEART

❧

Silence and Sharing around
the Word of God

✠ **THE LITURGICAL PRESS**
Collegeville, Minnesota

This printing for the United States of America and
Canada published by **The Liturgical Press**
Collegeville, Minnesota

Originally published as *Ecouter avec son coeur*
© Ateliers et Presses de Taizé 1992
Translation © Ateliers et Presses de Taizé 1992

Published in Great Britain by Geoffrey Chapman
Mowbray, a Cassell imprint
First published 1992

Library of Congress Cataloging-in-Publication Data
A catalog record for this book is available from the
Library of Congress.

ISBN 0-8146-2153-8

Scripture quotations are from the New Revised
Standard Version Bible, © 1989 by the Division of
Christian Education of the National Council of the
Churches of Christ in the USA. Used by permission.

Cover photograph: Sabine Nitzschke
Typeset by Litho Link Ltd, Welshpool, Powys, Wales
Printed and bound in Great Britain by
Biddles Ltd, Guildford and King's Lynn

INTRODUCTION

It was in the weekly meetings in Taizé that the 'Johannine hours' came into existence as times of silence and sharing around the Word of God. Why 'Johannine hours'? To try and listen, in the steps of the apostle John, to the voice of Christ. For John, perhaps more than for the other Biblical authors, being with Christ does not mean first of all acquiring knowledge, but recognizing the voice of the one our hearts love (see John 10.3–5).

But how can we read the Bible so as to hear the sound of Christ's voice? We need silence for this, because amidst the flood of words and noise that forces itself on us, the voice of Christ is quite soft. We also need to share, to communicate what we have heard and to listen to what others have understood. Nobody can grasp, all by themselves, all the fullness of Christ.

The idea of 'Johannine hours' grew out of a need for spiritual nourishment in the midst of daily life. Because of work or studies, it is often impossible to spend long hours in silence, but everyone can take an hour from time to time to enter a church, sit before an icon at home or go out into the solitude of nature. There, in silence, we can meditate on a passage of Scripture to listen to the voice of Christ.

Each double page of this book offers three elements for this meditation: a Bible text, a short commentary and some questions.

Another reason for the 'Johannine hours' is to foster a sharing. Concretely, this can happen in several ways. Some friends from the same parish or city can meet at the end of an afternoon to read aloud the Bible passage together; then they can spend an hour or two in silence and conclude with a brief sharing and a prayer. If everyone does not have the same two or three hours free, a day can be set aside when each person, at whatever hour they choose, can read the text and meditate on it in silence. In the evening, everyone can gather at the home of one of the participants or at the parish for a discussion and possibly a time of prayer. Others choose to read and reflect on the same Bible passage for an entire month, and then, when they have become very familiar with it, they meet for a time of sharing. Whatever form it takes, the important thing about the 'Johannine hours' is the complementarity between two elements—silence and sharing. The Word of God both touches the depth of the heart and gathers together in a fellowship.

During the time of silence, and even more during the group sharing, it is important to concentrate on what we understand and not waste time worrying if, in some Biblical expressions, we find it difficult to hear the voice of Christ. St John wrote: 'We declare to you what we have seen and heard . . . so that our joy may be complete' (1 John 1.3–4). Each person should say to themselves, concerning the sharing that concludes the 'Johannine hours', 'What I have understood and heard of Christ, that is what I want to communicate to others. I don't want to burden them with my own hesitations but rather tell them what has brought me joy, what has led me to run the risk of trusting more deeply.'

The Word of God has sometimes become an object of disputes. When that happens, the voice of Christ can no longer be heard; his word becomes inaccessible. Reading the Bible, instead of offering nourishment and vitality, instead of being a way of inner liberation, becomes a heavy burden to bear. Through the 'Johannine hours', we can discover the basic intuition of St John who writes that, from the beginning, the Word of God is Christ, and Christ alone (John 1.1, 9). Christ contains, interprets and enlightens the multiplicity of Bible texts.

A century after the time of the apostles, arguments and different opinions concerning Bible texts threatened to disconcert people's humble trust in God. Then Irenaeus of Lyons, who, in Asia Minor, had personally known a witness of the faith taught by John himself, wrote: 'Through the polyphony of texts, a single harmonious melody rings out within us, singing of the God who made all things' (*Adv. Haer.* 2, 28, 3). May the 'Johannine hours' allow us to hear that harmonious melody, which is none other than the voice of Christ who loves us. If we listen in our heart to the Word of God, and assimilate it in our life so as to put it into practice, then we will truly be blessed.

CONTENTS

1

The goodness of creation

GENESIS 1.1–5, 14–19, 26–28, 31 – 2.4

I N the beginning when God created the heavens and the earth, ²the earth was a formless void and darkness covered the face of the deep, while a wind from God swept over the face of the waters. ³Then God said, 'Let there be light'; and there was light. ⁴And God saw that the light was good; and God separated the light from the darkness. ⁵God called the light Day, and the darkness he called Night. And there was evening and there was morning, the first day.

¹⁴And God said, 'Let there be lights in the dome of the sky to separate the day from the night; and let them be for signs and for seasons and for days and years, ¹⁵and let them be lights in the dome of the sky to give light upon the earth.' And it was so. ¹⁶God made the two great lights—the greater light to rule the day and the lesser light to rule the night—and the stars. ¹⁷God set them in the dome of the sky to give light upon the earth, ¹⁸to rule over the day and over the night, and to separate the light from the darkness. And God saw that it was good. ¹⁹And there was evening and there was morning, the fourth day.

²⁶Then God said, 'Let us make humankind in our image, according to our likeness; and let them have dominion over the fish of the sea, and over the birds of the air, and over the cattle, and over all the wild animals of the earth, and over every creeping thing that creeps upon the earth.'

²⁷So God created humankind in his image,
in the image of God he created them;
male and female he created them.

²⁸God blessed them, and God said to them, 'Be fruitful and multiply, and fill the earth and subdue it; and have dominion over the fish of the sea and over the birds of the air and over every living thing that moves upon the earth.'

³¹God saw everything that he had made, and indeed, it was very good. And there was evening and there was morning, the sixth day.

¹Thus the heavens and the earth were finished, and all their multitude. ²And on the seventh day God finished the work that he had done, and he rested on the seventh day from all the work that he had done. ³So God blessed the seventh day and hallowed it, because on it God rested from all the work that he had done in creation.

⁴These are the generations of the heavens and the earth when they were created.

The author of the first creation story in the book of Genesis
did not lack audacity. He dared to go against ideas common in his
surroundings and assert that one God alone had created all things. For
Genesis, the sun and moon, the stars in the sky, which were revered by
other peoples as deities, are simply part of creation. A word of God
called them into being.

His boldness did not stop there. Other religions saw the
appearance of human beings on earth as the result of a misfortune, the
fall of a god. For Genesis, there is nothing like this. Human beings are
described as being in God's image, created by the deepest wish of the
Creator, who rejoices in giving and sharing: 'Let us make humankind
in our image' (Gen 1.26). This conviction leads the author to repeat
'God saw that it was good' and, after the creation of human beings, he
goes even further: 'God saw . . . and indeed, it was very good' (Gen 1.31).

Writing five or six centuries before Christ, the author could
not ignore human suffering, that which is undergone and that which is
caused. It is important for him, however, that his people meditate on
the pure source from which everything sprang forth and the way in
which God looks upon the human adventure, with trust and
wonderment. We have here a story that bears witness to the
astonishing intuitions of which faith is capable. We shall never know
what inner struggles its author had to wage within himself before
handing it down. The most striking messages of hope can be written
by people who have suffered and at first doubted.

Listening to this story today is a way of letting ourselves be
seized by the same trust God shows towards us. God says to each
person, 'Do you realize that you are a part of my creation which is
good? Through your existence, something unique and good enters into
the world.'

*How can the first creation story help us to accept our life as a gift and
something that is good?*
What helps us in this story in our struggle to overcome doubts and to believe?

2

An encounter with the living God

GENESIS 32.23–31

JACOB took his family and sent them across the stream, and likewise everything that he had. ²⁴Jacob was left alone; and a man wrestled with him until daybreak. ²⁵When the man saw that he did not prevail against Jacob, he struck him on the hip socket; and Jacob's hip was put out of joint as he wrestled with him. ²⁶Then he said, 'Let me go, for the day is breaking.' But Jacob said, 'I will not let you go, unless you bless me.' ²⁷So he said to him, 'What is your name?' And he said, 'Jacob.' ²⁸Then the man said, 'You shall no longer be called Jacob, but Israel, for you have striven with God and with humans, and have prevailed.' ²⁹Then Jacob asked him, 'Please tell me your name.' But he said, 'Why is it that you ask my name?' And there he blessed him. ³⁰So Jacob called the place Peniel, saying, 'For I have seen God face to face, and yet my life is preserved.' ³¹The sun rose upon him as he passed Penuel, limping because of his hip.

֍

Even if this age-old story is not fully understandable in all its details, it shows admirably the mysterious quality of an encounter with God. It is a critical moment in the life of the patriarch Jacob: he has just learnt that Esau, his brother from whom he stole the blessing of his father Isaac and who had threatened to kill him (Gen 27), is coming to meet him. To prepare himself for this formidable reunion, Jacob wants to be alone (vv. 23–24). And it is night.

In this vulnerable situation, Jacob encounters the Lord. But at the time he is not aware of this. His experience is one of wrestling the whole night long with 'a man' who refuses to tell him his name. Although apparently he wins the fight, he is marked for life (v. 25). And the stranger leaves him with two things: a new name and a blessing. In other words, this encounter reveals to him his true identity, and it is the source of a new life that will allow him to face an unpredictable future. Only afterwards does Jacob realize that he has met the living God in this experience of struggling in the dark.

How does this text help us to understand God's presence in our life and the consequences of this?

What does it mean for Jacob to receive a new name?

Have inner struggles helped me encounter the Lord in a new way?

3
Evil turned into good

GENESIS 50.15–21

REALIZING that their father was dead, Joseph's brothers said, 'What if Joseph still bears a grudge against us and pays us back in full for all the wrong that we did to him?' ¹⁶So they approached Joseph, saying, 'Your father gave this instruction before he died, ¹⁷"Say to Joseph: I beg you, forgive the crime of your brothers and the wrong they did in harming you." Now therefore please forgive the crime of the servants of the God of your father.' Joseph wept when they spoke to him. ¹⁸Then his brothers also wept, fell down before him, and said, 'We are here as your slaves.' ¹⁹But Joseph said to them, 'Do not be afraid! Am I in the place of God? ²⁰Even though you intended to do harm to me, God intended it for good, in order to preserve a numerous people, as he is doing today. ²¹So have no fear; I myself will provide for you and your little ones.' In this way he reassured them, speaking kindly to them.

Mistreated and sold into slavery in Egypt by his own brothers, Joseph eventually becomes the most powerful figure in Pharaoh's court, thanks to a series of surprising events. During a time of famine in many countries, Joseph organizes the food supply in Egypt so well that people come from all over to buy food.

One day, he sees his brothers arrive looking for provisions. Should he make them feel the seriousness of the wrong they did to him so that they will never do it again? Or is it possible to return good for evil? After a long inner struggle and a time of waiting that is very hard for his brothers, a reconciliation takes place. Joseph's whole family settles in Egypt and their lives are thus saved.

But since the wrong done to Joseph was so great, his brothers are still afraid of the consequences (vv. 15–18). So Joseph explains to them what their reconciliation was based on: 'Do not be afraid. Am I in the place of God? Even though you intended to do harm to me, God intended it for good' (vv. 19–20). And he points out that as a result of what has happened, many lives were saved. For Joseph, forgiving means not impeding God's loving designs and contributing one's own energies to bring them about.

How can we be peacemakers in a situation where evils that have been committed can lead to mistrust, fear and discouragement?

Can I trust that God, who by the resurrection transformed the sufferings of Christ into life for the world, will turn into good what has hurt me?

4

Return to the heart

DEUTERONOMY 30.11–14

S URELY, this commandment that I am commanding you today is not too hard for you, nor is it too far away. [12]It is not in heaven, that you should say, 'Who will go up to heaven for us, and get it for us so that we may hear it and observe it?' [13]Neither is it beyond the sea, that you should say, 'Who will cross to the other side of the sea for us, and get it for us so that we may hear it and observe it?' [14]No, the word is very near to you; it is in your mouth and in your heart for you to observe.

Who has not become exhausted by running after shining
mirages of ideals that could never become reality? The human
imagination constantly produces images of perfect situations where all
problems are solved. It says: do you see that perfect prayer, that
understanding of the faith, that Christian heroism that you could
attain? And then people start demanding this not just from themselves
but from others, too. 'If only they would live better and understand
more, we could go so far!'

Compared with all these demands that can never be
realized and that lead only to emptiness, the Word of God, expressing
the reality of God's love (that is what is meant by the 'Law'), brings us
back to what we are. God does not ask us to go up to heaven to
discover its mysteries. He does not require the exploit of crossing the
sea, something practically impossible in those days. The demands our
imagination makes on us push us and others beyond our resources and
our limits, where there is only the void, but God's Word is there where
we are. It invites us to return to our hearts just as they are, for it is
above all there that we encounter God.

The word is also 'in your mouth': that means, at a time
when people always read aloud, that the word read again and again
(Ps 1) becomes a simple means of communion with God.

*What demands do I make on myself that could lead me far away from myself
and from God?*
What words of the Gospel speak to my heart?

5
The call of God

1 SAMUEL 3.1–10

Now the boy Samuel was ministering to the Lord under Eli. The word of the Lord was rare in those days; visions were not widespread. ²At that time Eli, whose eyesight had begun to grow dim so that he could not see, was lying down in his room; ³the lamp of God had not yet gone out, and Samuel was lying down in the temple of the Lord, where the ark of God was. ⁴Then the Lord called, 'Samuel! Samuel!' and he said, 'Here I am!' ⁵and ran to Eli, and said, 'Here I am, for you called me.' But he said, 'I did not call; lie down again.' So he went and lay down. ⁶The Lord called again, 'Samuel!' Samuel got up and went to Eli, and said, 'Here I am, for you called me.' But he said, 'I did not call, my son; lie down again.' ⁷Now Samuel did not yet know the Lord, and the word of the Lord had not yet been revealed to him. ⁸The Lord called Samuel again, a third time. And he got up and went to Eli, and said, 'Here I am, for you called me.' Then Eli perceived that the Lord was calling the boy. ⁹Therefore Eli said to Samuel, 'Go, lie down; and if he calls you, you shall say, "Speak, Lord, for your servant is listening."' So Samuel went and lay down in his place.

¹⁰Now the Lord came and stood there, calling as before, 'Samuel! Samuel!' And Samuel said, 'Speak, for your servant is listening.'

Samuel is only a child. There is apparently nothing in the
way he acts to make us suspect that he is to receive a communication
from God. But one night, in bed, he hears someone calling him by
name. He is ready and willing to respond and so he goes to Eli the
priest, who had not called him. Only after this happens three times
does the young Samuel understand, with Eli's help, that it is God who
is calling. And so he replies, 'Speak, Lord, for your servant is listening.'

In the Bible, someone's name indicates their identity. God
alone is able to call us by our real name, since only God knows the
ground of our being. Indeed, his call is an invitation to discover our
true identity. It is a pressing invitation, as shown by the repetition of
the name ('Samuel, Samuel'), and one that is repeated, for God never
leaves us alone.

Sometimes we, too, when we hear the gentle echo of God's
call in the middle of our night, can mistake its origin. We try to
respond, but we do not know very well how to set about it. We are like
Jesus' disciples when they tell him that they do not know the way to
join him (cf. John 14.4–5).

It can therefore be essential for us to discover someone like
Eli, another believer, perhaps an elderly woman or man: a person who
can listen to us and help us decipher God's call deep within ourselves,
someone who can help us become what we are—servants of God.

Through what events is God calling me?
How can I better hear God's call?
Who has played the role of Eli in my life?
What does it mean for me to be a 'servant of God'?

6
Leave discouragement behind!

AHAB told Jezebel all that Elijah had done, and how he had killed all the prophets with the sword. ²Then Jezebel sent a messenger to Elijah, saying, 'So may the gods do to me, and more also, if I do not make your life like the life of one of them by this time tomorrow.' ³Then he was afraid; he got up and fled for his life, and came to Beersheba, which belongs to Judah; he left his servant there.

⁴But he himself went a day's journey into the wilderness, and came and sat down under a solitary broom tree. He asked that he might die: 'It is enough; now, O Lord, take away my life, for I am no better than my ancestors.' ⁵Then he lay down under the broom tree and fell asleep. Suddenly an angel touched him and said to him, 'Get up and eat.' ⁶He looked, and there at his head was a cake baked on hot stones, and a jar of water. He ate and drank, and lay down again. ⁷The angel of the Lord came a second time, touched him, and said, 'Get up and eat, otherwise the journey will be too much for you.' ⁸He got up, and ate and drank; then he went in the strength of that food forty days and forty nights to Horeb the mount of God. ⁹At that place he came to a cave, and spent the night there.

Then the word of the Lord came to him, saying, 'What are you doing here, Elijah?' ¹⁰He answered, 'I have been very zealous for the Lord, the God of hosts; for the Israelites have forsaken your covenant, thrown down your altars, and killed your prophets with the sword. I alone am left, and they are seeking my life, to take it away.'

¹¹He said, 'Go out and stand on the mountain before the Lord, for the Lord is about to pass by.' Now there was a great wind, so strong that it was splitting mountains and breaking rocks in pieces before the Lord, but the Lord was not in the wind; and after the wind an earthquake, but the Lord was not in the earthquake; ¹²and after the earthquake a fire, but the Lord was not in the fire; and after the fire a sound of sheer silence. ¹³When Elijah heard it, he wrapped his face in his mantle and went out and stood at the entrance of the cave. Then there came a voice to him.

⚘

These verses tell of a turning-point in the life of the prophet Elijah. The man of God had just been victorious in a bitter combat with his adversaries. To do this, he had to give himself to the end and risk everything, trusting in God. But then, when the queen threatens him with death, suddenly Elijah breaks down. He runs away and hides in the desert. Convinced of his worthlessness, he wishes only to die.

At that moment God's miracle takes place. Twice, a divine messenger wakes him up and gives him to eat and drink. Just as with the Israelites on the road to the Promised Land, God takes care of his chosen one when, humanly speaking, he is at the end of his rope. Elijah is thus enabled to set out on the road again and 'he went in the strength of that food forty days and forty nights to Horeb the mount of God'.

Because of this discovery of his own limits and of God's love for him, a love beyond anything he imagined, Elijah's life is deeply transformed. He becomes able to discern God's voice in a gentle breeze, a 'sound of sheer silence'. He has understood: God's victories have nothing in common with the powers of this world. God's designs are accomplished in discretion, and even in human weakness; faithfulness at all costs is more important than exploits that are as spectacular as they are short-lived.

Where in my life do I encounter the desert, in other words times and places where I feel the need for God more strongly?

How does God nourish me? What support does God give me for my pilgrimage of trust?

How can we hear the 'sound of sheer silence' by which God communicates with us?

Have human disappointments ever been for me a stepping-stone to a deeper relationship with God?

7

Happy the pure of heart

PSALM 51.1–17

Have mercy on me, O God,
    according to your steadfast love;
according to your abundant mercy
    blot out my transgressions.
²Wash me thoroughly from my iniquity,
    and cleanse me from my sin.
³For I know my transgressions,
    and my sin is ever before me.
⁴Against you, you alone, have I sinned,
    and done what is evil in your sight,
so that you are justified in your sentence
    and blameless when you pass judgement.
⁵Indeed, I was born guilty,
    a sinner when my mother conceived me.

⁶You desire truth in the inward being;
    therefore teach me wisdom in my secret heart.
⁷Purge me with hyssop, and I shall be clean;
    wash me, and I shall be whiter than snow.
⁸Let me hear joy and gladness;
    let the bones that you have crushed rejoice.
⁹Hide your face from my sins,
    and blot out all my iniquities.

¹⁰Create in me a clean heart, O God,
    and put a new and right spirit within me.
¹¹Do not cast me away from your presence,
    and do not take your holy spirit from me.
¹²Restore to me the joy of your salvation,
    and sustain in me a willing spirit.

¹³Then I will teach transgressors your ways,
    and sinners will return to you.
¹⁴Deliver me from bloodshed, O God,
    O God of my salvation,
    and my tongue will sing aloud of your deliverance.

¹⁵O Lord, open my lips,
    and my mouth will declare your praise.
¹⁶For you have no delight in sacrifice;
    if I were to give a burnt offering, you would not be pleased.
¹⁷The sacrifice acceptable to God is a broken spirit;
    a broken and contrite heart, O God, you will not despise.

This song of God's merciful love gives us a key for understanding Jesus' beatitude 'Blessed are the pure in heart . . .' (Matt 5.8). There is no danger that the psalmist may think that purity of heart is a consequence of human effort. On the contrary, he is very aware of his limits, of the lack of harmony between the reality of his life and what the Lord asks of him: 'My sin is ever before me' (v. 3). He knows too that what pleases God is not exterior ritual (v. 16) but rather 'truth in the inward being' (v. 6). From the heart, the depths of the being, all the rest of life flows (cf. Luke 6.43–45).

But how can we achieve this essential transparence of heart? For the psalmist, it can only be the work of God within him, the effect of God's 'steadfast love', his boundless goodness. Full of trust, he dares to pray in these words: 'Create in me a clean heart, O God . . .' (v. 10). God's forgiveness is thus revealed to be not just an attitude or feeling, but a creative act by which a new beginning becomes possible in the life of a human being (vv. 13–15).

Finally, the psalmist has this radiant intuition: 'The sacrifice acceptable to God is a broken spirit, a broken and contrite heart' (v. 17). This is not a doleful attitude, as it might seem at first sight; it does not involve belittling oneself or a wish for self-destruction. The person with a contrite heart is one who recognizes their own limits and who knows that they need God's continual mercy in order to live. A 'broken spirit' is the opposite of arrogant self-sufficiency; it implies availability and inward openness. In fact, it is the attitude of the tax collector in the Gospel parable of the Pharisee and the Tax Collector (Luke 18.9–14).

What biblical images or parables help us to understand better God's merciful love?

How can we root our lives in this merciful love?

In the psalm, a 'clean heart' and a 'broken heart' are two sides of the same reality: how can this be so?

8

A new song

O SING to the Lord a new song,
   for he has done marvellous things.
His right hand and his holy arm
   have gotten him victory.
²The Lord has made known his victory;
   he has revealed his vindication in the sight of the nations.
³He has remembered his steadfast love and faithfulness
   to the house of Israel.
All the ends of the earth have seen
   the victory of our God.

⁴Make a joyful noise to the Lord, all the earth;
   break forth into joyous song and sing praises.
⁵Sing praises to the Lord with the lyre,
   with the lyre and the sound of melody.
⁶With trumpets and the sound of the horn
   make a joyful noise before the King, the Lord.

⁷Let the sea roar, and all that fills it;
   the world and those who live in it.
⁸Let the floods clap their hands;
   let the hills sing together for joy
⁹at the presence of the Lord, for he is coming
   to judge the earth.
He will judge the world with righteousness,
   and the peoples with equity.

If the basic vocation of human beings is to praise God, it is nonetheless true that very few of our songs are fit for this praise. The reality of our human condition, with its load of disappointments and impossibilities, weighs us down and wears us out. Where can a source of renewal be found which would enable us to hope again and again?

The answer of ancient Israel to this question was: by recalling the 'marvellous things' of God, the deeds by which he showed his love by saving his people from death. Through the exodus from Egypt, through the return from captivity in Babylon, God revealed his faithful love for his people in the sight of all the nations. And so the psalmist can invite the whole of creation to sing a new song, a hymn of thanksgiving for the presence and activity of God at the heart of creation.

For the Christian, this vision of reality finds a fulfilment in the coming—and especially in the resurrection—of our Lord Jesus Christ. By sending his Son into the world and by saving him from the power of death, God 'judges the world with righteousness', in other words he makes clearly visible, in the midst of our world, his love and all the consequences that it entails. This 'judgement' is neither a definitive condemnation nor an impossible ideal made into a law: it becomes a concrete reality for us in the gift of the Holy Spirit 'without measure' (cf. John 3.34). All are thus offered an inward re-creation which gives a new way of looking at events. In this way, all people can praise the Lord in a fitting way; from their 'new hearts' will rise up a song that is truly new because it constantly overcomes the downward pull of evil.

By what 'marvellous things' does God reveal his love and justice today?
What enables us to live in constant gratefulness, to keep a 'new song' alive in our hearts?

9
A spirit of childhood

PSALM 131

O LORD, my heart is not lifted up,
my eyes are not raised too high;
I do not occupy myself with things
too great and too marvellous for me.
²But I have calmed and quieted my soul,
like a weaned child with its mother;
my soul is like the weaned child that is with me.

³O Israel, hope in the Lord
from this time on and for evermore.

This little psalm sums up admirably the basic attitude of a believer in the image of a little child on its mother's lap. We are familiar with the image of a child from the preaching of Jesus (cf. Matt 18.1–4; Mark 10.13–16) and so we are in danger of being a bit too accustomed to it, of missing its astonishing, even revolutionary, character.

The attitude of humility or spiritual poverty that we find in this psalm is the result of a long evolution in the Bible. It does not come from the rejection of the things of this earth: 'God saw everything that he had made, and it was very good' (Gen 1.31). And this is true above all of human beings made in God's image (Gen 1.27). They are invited to enjoy the good things of creation, to put their talents to use and to fulfil their possibilities. In itself, wealth is thus seen as a blessing.

At the same time, since the exodus from Egypt the people of God realized that God had a special concern for the needy and downtrodden. When they were nothing but a bunch of slaves, the Lord had liberated them and made them his own people. And each time they cried to God in their distress, they were convinced that God would open a way forward for them.

Gradually, it became clear to some people that too much confidence in one's own qualities or possessions could hinder a person from welcoming God's gifts. How could God fill hands that were already full by their own efforts? The only road, then, was to remain in an attitude of trusting openness, to view everything as a sheer gift of God's goodness. Turning to God rather than trying to find a way out by one's own cleverness was found to be the only way to see still greater things (John 1.50) and to receive the whole world as an inheritance (Rom 4.13; cf. Matt 5.3–5).

How does the image of a child on its mother's lap help me to understand who God is and my own relationship with God?

How can I 'calm and quiet' my soul?

10

A life beyond all our hopes

S EEK the Lord while he may be found,
   call upon him while he is near;
let the wicked forsake their way,
   and the unrighteous their thoughts;
let them return to the Lord, that he may have mercy on them,
   and to our God, for he will abundantly pardon.
⁸For my thoughts are not your thoughts,
   nor are your ways my ways, says the Lord.
⁹For as the heavens are higher than the earth,
   so are my ways higher than your ways
   and my thoughts than your thoughts.

¹⁰For as the rain and the snow come down from heaven,
   and do not return there until they have watered the earth,
making it bring forth and sprout,
   giving seed to the sower and bread to the eater,
¹¹so shall my word be that goes out from my mouth;
   it shall not return to me empty,
but it shall accomplish that which I purpose,
   and succeed in the thing for which I sent it.

¹²For you shall go out in joy,
   and be led back in peace;
the mountains and the hills before you
   shall burst into song,
   and all the trees of the field shall clap their hands.
¹³Instead of the thorn shall come up the cypress;
   instead of the brier shall come up the myrtle;
and it shall be to the Lord for a memorial,
   for an everlasting sign that shall not be cut off.

The whole 'Book of Consolation' (Isa 40 – 55) is a call to
God's people to take a new step and to discover broader horizons in
their life in God. They seem to have reasons to be disappointed in their
God: the Temple has been destroyed, the Promised Land devastated,
the time of exile has come. God has not kept his promises!

From within your horizon you are right, the prophet tells
his people. But God's horizon is much wider! And his greatness lies in
the fact that he remains close, even when no support is found in
external realities. God will keep his promise beyond all our hopes, as
surely as the rain causes seeds to grow and allows the land to return
grain to the sower.

Every believer is called to pass through similar experiences.
Trusting that God lets himself be found in the present can seem to be a
poor message in the face of the sometimes cruel events we live
through. Yet this message bears within it the power of a life beyond all
our hopes. It opens a road through our deserts, a road that lets us go
beyond ourselves. We are no longer forced to rely only on our own
resources; we participate in the mysterious destiny of the 'Servant of
God' who, 'despised and rejected by others' (53.3), became the 'light
to the nations' (49.6).

As we set out on this road, we are already given a glimpse
of a joy that will spring forth. All of nature will share in it as part of a
new creation. On this road we shall find ourselves in the company of
many others. 'A people yet unborn will praise the Lord' (Ps 102.18).

*How can I keep on trusting in God's promise, even when it is no longer
possible to rely on external things?*

*In what situations in my life have I realized that God is greater
than all that I had known of him before, and that he was listening to me in a
different way than I expected?*

11
Arise, shine!

ISAIAH 60.1–5

A RISE, shine; for your light has come,
   and the glory of the Lord has risen upon you.
²For darkness shall cover the earth,
   and thick darkness the peoples;
but the Lord will arise upon you,
   and his glory will appear over you.
³Nations shall come to your light,
   and kings to the brightness of your dawn.

⁴Lift up your eyes and look around;
   they all gather together, they come to you;
your sons shall come from far away,
   and your daughters shall be carried on their nurses' arms.
⁵Then you shall see and be radiant;
   your heart shall thrill and rejoice,
because the abundance of the sea shall be brought to you,
   the wealth of the nations shall come to you.

This passage from Isaiah dates from a time when discouragement threatened the people of God. The city of Jerusalem, centre and high point for a public celebration of God, had been rebuilt after the destruction of wartime, but it never regained its past splendour and renown.

The prophet receives a glimpse of what God intends for his city: it is time for her to rise up, to shine by welcoming God's light with joy. God wishes to be himself the light of his people (v. 19).

From the very beginning, Christians saw in these words a promise for the Church. She dares to make herself beautiful (Rev 21.2) to welcome generously, to be a light in the darkness of peoples. And since the Church comes to life within each of us, in the yes our heart speaks to the Christ of communion, the words 'Arise, shine!' are meant for us as well.

What does this passage tell us about that mystery of communion which is the Church?

What can the words 'Arise, shine!' mean in our life, and how can we rejoice in what God is accomplishing in and through us?

12

The wisdom of the poor

JEREMIAH 9.23–24

THUS says the Lord: Do not let the wise boast in their wisdom, do not let the mighty boast in their might, do not let the wealthy boast in their wealth; [24]but let those who boast boast in this, that they understand and know me, that I am the Lord; I act with steadfast love, justice, and righteousness in the earth, for in these things I delight, says the Lord.

In the final analysis, where do we find our security? In whom or what do we place our trust? The prophet Jeremiah had to deal with these questions at a critical moment in the life of his people. All round him, he saw his compatriots counting upon their gifts of intelligence or strength, or on their possessions. Personally, the prophet had nothing against these human realities, but he realized that the time would come when they would no longer suffice for the people to cope with their situation, to find a meaning in their life. Night would fall, when human hands and eyes would no longer be of use, when certainties would vanish. Then, all that would be left would be the rock of knowledge of God.

What is this knowledge so essential for life? For Jeremiah, it is an attitude of the heart, with nothing theoretical about it. It is rooted in the depths of the human being, and involves a basic choice, a saying yes with one's whole life. Knowledge of God leads directly to a way of life, to doing good (cf. Jer 4.22), to taking care of those in need (22.15f.).

How can the knowledge of God be acquired? Jeremiah knows that, when all is said and done, it is a gift from God (24.7), since God alone can transform human hearts. Our role is to welcome this gift by an attitude of trust. Only this trust enables us to go forward in the darkest hours of the night, to discern in the events of the world and of our lives the face of a God who 'acts with steadfast love, justice, and righteousness on earth'.

Where do I find security? How can I view my personal qualities not as ways of justifying or defending myself but as gifts of God that must grow and bear fruit?

How can I penetrate beneath the surface of events to discern what God is accomplishing in my own life and in the human family?

13
A breath of life

THE hand of the Lord came upon me, and he brought me out by the spirit of the Lord and set me down in the middle of a valley; it was full of bones. ²He led me all around them; there were very many lying in the valley, and they were very dry. ³He said to me, 'Mortal, can these bones live?' I answered, 'O Lord God, you know.' ⁴Then he said to me, 'Prophesy to these bones, and say to them: O dry bones, hear the word of the Lord. ⁵Thus says the Lord God to these bones: I will cause breath to enter you, and you shall live. ⁶I will lay sinews on you, and will cause flesh to come upon you, and cover you with skin, and put breath in you, and you shall live; and you shall know that I am the Lord.'

⁷So I prophesied as I had been commanded; and as I prophesied, suddenly there was a noise, a rattling, and the bones came together, bone to its bone. ⁸I looked, and there were sinews on them, and flesh had come upon them, and skin had covered them; but there was no breath in them. ⁹Then he said to me, 'Prophesy to the breath, prophesy, mortal, and say to the breath: Thus says the Lord God: Come from the four winds, O breath, and breathe upon these slain, that they may live.' ¹⁰I prophesied as he commanded me, and the breath came into them, and they lived, and stood on their feet, a vast multitude.

¹¹Then he said to me, 'Mortal, these bones are the whole house of Israel. They say, "Our bones are dried up, and our hope is lost; we are cut off completely." ¹²Therefore prophesy, and say to them, Thus says the Lord God: I am going to open your graves, and bring you up from your graves, O my people; and I will bring you back to the land of Israel. ¹³And you shall know that I am the Lord, when I open your graves, and bring you up from your graves, O my people. ¹⁴I will put my spirit within you, and you shall live, and I will place you on your own soil; then you shall know that I, the Lord, have spoken and will act, says the Lord.'

꧁

At a very difficult time for God's people, when the nation is destroyed and its rulers in exile far from home, a prophet has a vision that reveals God's identity and his desires for those he loves. He sees a valley filled with human bones lying on the ground. And then, when the prophet begins to proclaim the word of God to these dry bones, all at once they start to come together. The breath of life enters them and they turn into a great multitude of living human beings.

Through this vision, God reveals himself to his people as the source of their life and the motive force of their history. Discouraged, the faithful had thought they had no future and no hope. They felt like the living dead. But no, says the prophet: God, Creator of the world and Ruler of history, is able to bring life even in places where there is only death and despair. By the Spirit, God's own breath of life, we shall be able to set out again with new vitality. In this way, God shows his identity: the God who gives life in order to display his great mercy.

Are there periods in our life when we are like 'dry bones'? How can we remain open in such situations to the breath of God's Spirit?

How does God's word come to us in order to transform our life, to give us new vitality?

14
The wonder of a love

HOSEA 11.1–4, 7–9

W HEN Israel was a child, I loved him,
  and out of Egypt I called my son.
²The more I called them,
    the more they went from me;
they kept sacrificing to the Baals,
    and offering incense to idols.

³Yet it was I who taught Ephraim to walk,
    I took them up in my arms;
    but they did not know that I healed them.
⁴I led them with cords of human kindness,
    with bands of love.
I was to them like those
    who lift infants to their cheeks.
    I bent down to them and fed them.

⁷My people are bent on turning away from me.
    To the Most High they call,
    but he does not raise them up at all.

⁸How can I give you up, Ephraim?
    How can I hand you over, O Israel?
My heart recoils within me;
    my compassion grows warm and tender.
⁹I will not execute my fierce anger;
    I will not again destroy Ephraim;
for I am God and no mortal,
    the Holy One in your midst,
    and I will not come in wrath.

Eight centuries before Christ, the prophet Hosea grasped the absolute nature of God's love. He understood that God loves with a love which will not be stopped even if it meets with a refusal.

By freeing his people from slavery in Egypt, God showed his love. Then he drew close like a father or mother 'bending down and feeding them' (v. 4). God cannot bear the pain of seeing the distress of his people who are stricken by violence. Instead of turning to him, they cling to their refusal like an electrocuted person who cannot let go of the electric wire that is endangering their life.

Nothing hurts as much as being forgotten by those one loves. With human beings, this pain can easily turn into anger and the desire for revenge. But when God is rejected and forgotten, his searing pain does not become inflamed with hatred, but with compassion. 'For', says God, 'I am God and no mortal, the Holy One in your midst' (v. 9). God's holiness is the love which never says: I've had enough. Once God has committed himself to his people, his love is so strong that he cannot cease to love.

What touches me the most about the love God has for us?

How can we respond to God who waits for us always, even when he is rejected?

15

Come back to God

HOSEA 14.1–8

Rᴇᴛᴜʀɴ, O Israel, to the Lord your God,
 for you have stumbled because of your iniquity.
²Take words with you
   and return to the Lord;
say to him,
   'Take away all guilt;
accept that which is good,
   and we will offer
   the fruit of our lips.
³Assyria shall not save us;
   we will not ride upon horses;
we will say no more, "Our God",
   to the work of our hands.
In you the orphan finds mercy.'

⁴I will heal their disloyalty;
   I will love them freely,
   for my anger has turned from them.
⁵I will be like the dew to Israel;
   he shall blossom like the lily,
   he shall strike root like the forests of Lebanon.
⁶His shoots shall spread out;
   his beauty shall be like the olive tree,
   and his fragrance like that of Lebanon.
⁷They shall again live beneath my shadow,
   they shall flourish as a garden;
they shall blossom like the vine,
   their fragrance shall be like the wine of Lebanon.

⁸O Ephraim, what have I to do with idols?
   It is I who answer and look after you.
I am like an evergreen cypress;
   your faithfulness comes from me.

'I will love them freely' (v. 4). God loves his people with a love that is given without conditions or ulterior motives, a serene love. He had sought to draw them close to him by bonds of love. Pained by their indifference or even at times their refusal, he called them passionately to come back to him. Now, it is as if he were speaking only to himself. No more vibrant calls to conversion, no more 'Thus says the Lord'. In this silence of God, the prophet alone has heard the irrevocable decision: 'I love them; I will fall upon them like dew.'

Thus the prophet calls quite simply for a return to God. He asks for nothing difficult, no sacrifices or guilty consciences. God's love has shown itself to be so trustworthy in his eyes that there is no need to insist. Each person can come to God as they are and say 'Take away all guilt; accept that which is good' (v. 2). God has compassion on all those who are ill because they have been disappointed and abandoned, who have no strength to get up and begin again.

Whoever consents, before all else, to being loved by God is filled to overflowing with the beauty of the lily, the strength of the poplar and the splendour of the olive tree. In the sight of God (v. 7), they will become fruitful.

What enables me to return to God in all simplicity, like a child?
How can I rejoice at the beauty that God gives to my life and the lives of others?

16
Searching with confidence

MATTHEW 6.25–34

'THEREFORE I tell you, do not worry about your life, what you will eat or what you will drink, or about your body, what you will wear. Is not life more than food, and the body more than clothing? [26]Look at the birds of the air; they neither sow nor reap nor gather into barns, and yet your heavenly Father feeds them. Are you not of more value than they? [27]And can any of you by worrying add a single hour to your span of life? [28]And why do you worry about clothing? Consider the lilies of the field, how they grow; they neither toil, nor spin, [29]yet I tell you, even Solomon in all his glory was not clothed like one of these. [30]But if God so clothes the grass of the field, which is alive today and tomorrow is thrown into the oven, will he not much more clothe you— you of little faith? [31]Therefore do not worry, saying, "What will we eat?" or "What will we drink?" or "What will we wear?" [32]For it is the Gentiles who strive for all these things; and indeed your heavenly Father knows that you need all these things. [33]But strive first for the kingdom of God and his righteousness, and all these things will be given to you as well.

[34]"So do not worry about tomorrow, for tomorrow will bring worries of its own. Today's trouble is enough for today.'

❧

A call to search can inspire different reactions. Some will respond with anxiety: will I manage? What if I do not find anything? Or if I do not search in the right way?

It is striking to see how positive the notion of seeking is for Christ. For him, it is never linked to despair or worry. That is why in the very same passage he can say to his disciples 'Don't worry' (vv. 25, 34) and then add immediately afterwards: 'Seek' (v. 33).

Don't worry . . . but seek. If Jesus speaks in this way, that is because the object of the search is already given. The realities of God are not inaccessible; they are present, close at hand, and Jesus explains why: 'Do not be afraid, little flock, for it is your Father's good pleasure to give you the Kingdom' (Luke 12.32). Seeking means first of all looking with Christ toward the One who is pleased to give. It means realizing that God does not give a snake to whoever asks for a fish, or a scorpion to whoever asks for an egg (Luke 11.9–13).

For Jesus, confident trust and searching are not opposed. The call not to worry does not put us to sleep; the invitation to search never sets us on the road of fear. The confidence that we shall find drives out anxiety and, instead of causing worry, searching can become, again and again, a joyful adventure.

Our ability to trust is often wounded and hesitating. What does God offer us to heal us and to turn our life and our searching into a creation with him?

17
Confident waiting

MATTHEW 13.24–30

J ESUS put before them another parable: 'The kingdom of heaven may be compared to someone who sowed good seed in his field; ²⁵but while everybody was asleep, an enemy came and sowed weeds among the wheat, and then went away. ²⁶So when the plants came up and bore grain, then the weeds appeared as well. ²⁷And the slaves of the householder came and said to him, "Master, did you not sow good seed in your field? Where, then, did these weeds come from?" ²⁸He answered, "An enemy has done this." The slaves said to him, "Then do you want us to go and gather them?" ²⁹But he replied, "No; for in gathering the weeds you would uproot the wheat along with them. ³⁰Let both of them grow together until the harvest; and at harvest time I will tell the reapers, Collect the weeds first and bind them in bundles to be burned, but gather the wheat into my barn."'

꧑

Several times, Christ compares the kingdom of heaven,
which already has begun on earth by God's presence and the continual
activity of his Spirit, to the action of sowing seeds, to a growth
process, to a harvest. But while sowing and harvesting are stages that
can be observed, the long and essential period of growth is more
mysterious. The hasty eye does not discern, in the apparent inactivity
of a sown field, the continuous approach of an abundant harvest.

For the one who does see, a question or even a doubt can
still arise: how is it that whenever God's Spirit is at work there are also
so many incomprehensible and contradictory events? Jesus sowed the
good seed of forgiveness; where then do the disputes between those
who bear his name come from? Christ's Spirit lives in me; where then
does all that is unbearable in me come from?

In this parable, it is an enemy of the owner of the field who
sows the weeds to get back at him; we are not told why. In the Gospel,
Christ and his mission are threatened from the very beginning: by the
murderous anger of Herod who kills children with impunity, then bv
the sly suggestions of the Tempter who tries to keep Christ from
trusting in God alone.

Threats to the life of God in us are not removed by
precipitate action that tries to tear out all evil, but rather by trust,
like that of the owner in the parable. He knows that nothing that is
good will be lost, and that the rest—the weeds that will already be dry
and burnt before the grain is gathered—will no longer be remembered
when the joy of harvest-time comes.

*Which events and situations leave us disconcerted and asking: 'Where did
these weeds come from?' (v. 27).*

*Who is for me like the owner of the field in the parable, whose trust calms
worry and makes it possible to persevere with patience?*

18

The hidden presence of God's Kingdom

J ESUS put before them another parable: 'The kingdom of heaven is like a mustard seed that someone took and sowed in his field; [12]it is the smallest of all the seeds, but when it has grown it is the greatest of shrubs and becomes a tree, so that the birds of the air come and make nests in its branches.'

[33]He told them another parable: 'The kingdom of heaven is like yeast that a woman took and mixed in with three measures of flour until all of it was leavened.'

꿎

Two parables with the same theme, one taken from a
man's work, the other from a woman's.

The tree that shelters the birds of the air is an image of a
universal welcome: 'People will come from east and west, from north
and south, and will eat in the kingdom of God' (Luke 13.29). God
brings about his loving designs for all peoples by means of realities
that resemble a mustard seed: humble prayer, forgiveness received and
offered, a simple welcome. Elsewhere in the Gospel, the mustard seed
is an image of faith. When the apostles ask Christ to increase their
faith, he replies that trust as big as a mustard seed is all that is needed
(Luke 17.5–6).

Although the plant that grows from the mustard seed has a
precise size, the same thing cannot be said of leaven. As soon as it is
mixed into the dough, its field of action cannot be circumsized. The
presence of the Spirit of Christ may be discreet like this, but it leavens
all that it penetrates so that in the end 'God may be all in all'
(1 Cor 15.28).

*Where have I seen the humble presence of God's Kingdom—for example, in
the kindness of a human heart or in an act of reconciliation or sharing—
become a place of welcome and communion for many?*

*Instead of passing judgement from the outside, how can we be a leaven that
works from within?*

19
Don't be afraid, I am here

IMMEDIATELY Jesus made the disciples get into the boat and go on ahead to the other side, while he dismissed the crowds. ²³And after he had dismissed dismissed the crowds, he went up the mountain by himself to pray. When evening came, he was there alone, ²⁴but by this time the boat, battered by the waves, was far from the land, for the wind was against them. ²⁵And early in the morning he came walking toward them on the sea. ²⁶But when the disciples saw him walking on the sea, they were terrified, saying, 'It is a ghost!' And they cried out in fear. ²⁷But immediately Jesus spoke to them and said, 'Take heart, it is I; do not be afraid.'

²⁸Peter answered him, 'Lord, if it is you, command me to come to you on the water.' ²⁹He said, 'Come.' So Peter got out of the boat, started walking on the water, and came toward Jesus. ³⁰But when he noticed the strong wind, he became frightened, and beginning to sink, he cried out, 'Lord, save me!' ³¹Jesus immediately reached out his hand and caught him, saying to him, 'You of little faith, why did you doubt?' ³²When they got into the boat, the wind ceased. ³³And those in the boat worshipped him saying, 'Truly you are the Son of God.'

෨

For the people of the Bible, the sea is often a symbol of the power of death or of the forces of chaos in the world. To show Jesus walking upon the sea expresses the fact that he has overcome death and the chaos in the world. It already reveals his identity as the Risen Lord.

Is it possible, in this world, to share in Christ's life and all it represents? Such appears to be Peter's desire, and to this desire Jesus simply replies, 'Come' (v. 29). A single word to say that the way is open, accessible for all who want to follow him.

Entering now into the life of resurrection means entering into something radically new. No previous experience can serve as a reference-point. It is a life of trust in God. Affirming that Jesus has overcome death and the forces of chaos is not based on visible proof. Do we see it in the world? So many things incline us to believe the contrary — war, hatred, mindless violence, evil in all its shapes and forms . . . Only by keeping our eyes fixed on Christ are we able to discern this truth.

Peter starts to sink the moment his eyes look away from Christ and see the strength of the wind and the height of the waves. Fear grips him. But when Peter sinks beneath the waves, crying out, 'Lord, save me!', the Gospel shows us something important. Not a heroic act by Peter, but rather an act of Christ: 'Jesus immediately reached out his hand and caught him.' What can we learn from this? First of all this: every commitment to follow Christ is based not on our strength but on Christ's faithfulness; he rescued Peter when Peter's faith gave way. If Christ asks us a question when we want to go with him in his life of resurrection, the question he asks is not 'Are you sure of your strength, sure you have enough faith?' He asks us a quite different question, much less centred on ourselves: 'Do you believe I will be at your side? Do you believe in my faithfulness?'

How can we come to realize more clearly that our commitments, especially a lifelong commitment because of Christ, rest on God's faithfulness?
What helps me to keep my eyes fixed on Christ?

20
Saying yes

MATTHEW 21.28–31

JESUS said, 'What do you think? A man had two sons; he went to the first and said, "Son, go and work in the vineyard today." ²⁹He answered, "I will not"; but later he changed his mind and went. ³⁰The father went to the second and said the same; and he answered, "I go, sir"; but he did not go. ³¹Which of the two did the will of his father?' They said, 'The first.' Jesus said to them, 'Truly I tell you, the tax collectors and the prostitutes are going into the kingdom of God ahead of you.'

≈

Every human being has heard a call from God. But in this parable of the two sons, the story does not include a person who, after hearing the call, says yes at once and then does what is asked. Christ is fully familiar with the tortuous ways of the human heart, and so he speaks only of the person who says yes and does nothing, and of the other one who at first refuses but then does the will of his father.

What matters is not our first reaction to God's call, but the courage not to justify our own unwillingness. In daily life—and this parable takes an example from ordinary life—it could seem humiliating to do what we had earlier refused to do. Except for a child who knows that he will not have to explain or justify why it was first no, then yes. God will never ask this of us; he is not offended by our inability to say yes straightaway. God's only desire is that his loving will be done.

Where can we find the simplicity of heart not to be bound by our prior refusals?
How can I discover what I really want, in the depths of my heart?

21
Watch and pray

MATTHEW 26.36–44

T HEN Jesus went with them to a place called Gethsemane; and he said to his disciples, 'Sit here while I go over there and pray.' ³⁷He took with him Peter and the two sons of Zebedee, and began to be grieved and agitated. ³⁸Then he said to them, 'I am deeply grieved, even to death; remain here, and stay awake with me.' ³⁹And going a little farther, he threw himself on the ground and prayed, 'My father, if it is possible, let this cup pass from me; yet not what I want but what you want.' ⁴⁰Then he came to the disciples and found them sleeping; and he said to Peter, 'So, could you not stay awake with me one hour? ⁴¹Stay awake and pray that you may not come into the time of trial; the spirit indeed is willing, but the flesh is weak.' ⁴²Again he went away for the second time and prayed, 'My Father, if this cannot pass unless I drink it, your will be done.' ⁴³Again he came and found them sleeping, for their eyes were heavy. ⁴⁴So leaving them again, he went away and prayed for the third time, saying the same words.

At the beginning of the sombre events leading to the death of Jesus, the gospel writers give us a glimpse of his inner combat. There, even before he falls into the hands of his enemies, the essential of his redemptive work is played out. Jesus gives his life freely, before the soldiers take him by force, but first he has to experience in his very flesh what the authentic use of freedom entails (cf. Heb 5.8). In this way, in his human existence, he reveals to us God's love in its most personal dimension.

In the solitude of Gethsemane, Jesus is confronted by the immensity of evil, the refusal of light and communion, as something he has to pass through. He experiences the horror of this, and an extreme aversion which has less to do with his human weakness than with the incompatibility between evil and the God of goodness and life. He takes up into his relationship with the Father the tormenting question of the just person who is being persecuted: 'How is it possible for the way of the Lord to pass through the dark night of evil?'

Jesus finds a way out of this seemingly hopeless situation by an act of trust made in utter darkness. This trust expresses a certainty: God is still his Abba, his loving Father, who wants what is best for him and for the world; he is never the author or the accomplice of evil. God's will is thus a source of life, even when this seems to be belied by appearances. Jesus' yes to this will, a yes that is totally poor yet rooted in filial trust, opens a space for the love of God in the midst of the weaknesses of the human condition—and its refusals—in order to make healing possible.

In what way does Christ's attitude on the Mount of Olives help me to cope with moments of trial and doubt in my life?
How can we wake from our sleep in order to 'watch and pray' with Christ?

22
Confidence in the vitality of the Gospel

MARK 4.1–9

A GAIN Jesus began to teach beside the sea. Such a very large crowd gathered around him that he got into a boat on the sea and sat there, while the whole crowd was beside the sea on the land. ²He began to teach them many things in parables, and in his teaching he said to them: ³'Listen! A sower went out to sow. ⁴And as he sowed, some seed fell on the path, and the birds came and ate it up. ⁵Other seed fell on rocky ground, where it did not have much soil, and it sprang up quickly, since it had no depth of soil. ⁶And when the sun rose, it was scorched; and since it had no root, it withered away. ⁷Other seed fell among thorns, and the thorns grew up and choked it, and it yielded no grain. ⁸Other seed fell into good soil and brought forth grain, growing up and increasing and yielding thirty and sixty and a hundredfold.' ⁹And he said, 'Let anyone with ears to hear listen!'

When Jesus speaks in a parable about sowing and the gradual growth of the wheat, he is speaking of a reality familiar to all his listeners. We can easily imagine the farmers of Galilee nodding their heads with understanding as he describes difficulties like stony ground, brambles and birds eating up the freshly sown seed.

But Jesus draws our attention to something else that could easily be overlooked. He points out that the birds, stones and thorns do not count for much in the face of the life-force which is in the seeds and which results in a good harvest even though not all the soil in the field is good. The sower who has sown generously without worrying too much where the seed fell has nothing to fear; at harvest-time there will be an abundant crop.

'The secret of the kingdom of God' (Mark 4.11) has a dimension that is visible and known to all; from the time of Jesus down to the present day, the Gospel has been widely proclaimed, openly, in both favourable and unfavourable situations. And just as the loss of the seeds which fall on the wayside is noticed before the harvest which will come from the good soil, so also the indifference or superficial welcome which the Gospel has often encountered is visible before the harvest which comes where it has been accepted with generosity.

Jesus' parable helps us see something which, because it is not immediately apparent, could be easily overlooked: in the Gospel there is a life-force, the Holy Spirit, which produces a good harvest in all the good soil it finds. The Word of the Gospel comes to live deep within every human being. Jesus' parable calls us to place our trust in the Gospel as a word which creates.

What does this parable tell us about the way in which God is bringing his Kingdom about in our world?

What harvest has the Gospel, sown by Christ and by the whole Church, already produced in those around me, in my own life, in the history of the world and that of my own country?

23

Who am I for you?

J ESUS went on with his disciples to the villages of Caesarea Philippi; and on the way he asked his disciples, 'Who do people say that I am?' [28]And they answered him, 'John the Baptist; and others, Elijah; and still others, one of the prophets.' [29]He asked them, 'But who do you say that I am?' Peter answered him, 'You are the Messiah.' [30]And he sternly ordered them not to tell anyone about him.

In the Gospel, Jesus often asks questions. He asks, 'Why are you afraid?' (Mark 4.40) or, when many forsake him, he asks the apostles, 'Do you also wish to go away?' (John 6.67). Later, he asks Peter, 'Do you love me?' (John 21.15). At a decisive moment in his life on earth, when it will become clear whether or not those closest to him at least will be able to recognize who he is, Jesus does not make a statement about his identity; he asks a question.

There lies one of the mysteries regarding Christ's being: he adopts to such an extent an attitude of self-giving, he becomes so poor and humble that the revelation of his identity does not come about through an affirmation, but by an answer to his questions. The free response that human beings are called to give to God is the only thing over which he has no power. By asking through his life and his words the question 'Who am I for you?', Christ places himself entirely in human hands. He can do nothing about the great diversity of opinions about him, but for whoever turns to him and recognizes him, he is the radiant reflection of God, the one and only way.

What question is Christ asking me today in the depths of my heart?

How can I find the courage to respond, not with something that is just one opinion among others about Christ, but with a response that commits my life?

24

Coming to God as we are

P EOPLE were bringing little children to Jesus in order that he might touch them; and the disciples spoke sternly to them. [14]But when Jesus saw this, he was indignant and said to them, 'Let the little children come to me; do not stop them; for it is to such as these that the kingdom of God belongs. [15]Truly I tell you, whoever does not receive the kingdom of God as a little child will never enter it.' [16]And he took them up in his arms, laid his hands on them, and blessed them.

In the time of Jesus, it was customary for people to ask noted religious teachers to bless their children. Here these parents ask Jesus not just for a blessing (which could remain purely formal); they want him to touch their children. It is easy to imagine the disciples' astonishment when Jesus becomes indignant at their well-meaning attempt to send these people away so that they will not disturb him. Jesus not only welcomes the children and blesses them; he goes even further, embracing them.

Jesus' indignation is a sign that the heart of the Gospel is at stake. Jesus embraces the children to make this still more evident. Did he do this because the children deserved it? No, Jesus says nothing about their merits. If God gives all his love to children (the Kingdom of God belongs to them, v. 14), that means that this love is offered to each one of us, unconditionally. We can therefore come to God just as we are. The only thing said about the children is that they are brought, carried, to Jesus (v. 13). This does not speak about their strong points, but rather about their powerlessness. For it is in our weakness that God wishes to welcome us (cf. Luke 15.20).

What helps us to realize that, in God's sight, we do not have to pretend that we are more than we are, that we can be like children before God?

How can we know that, in spite of our contradictions, we are already 'children of God'?

25

Mary's Yes

I N the sixth month the angel Gabriel was sent by God to a town in Galilee called Nazareth, ²⁷to a virgin engaged to a man whose name was Joseph, of of the house of David. The virgin's name was Mary. ²⁸And he came to her and said, 'Greetings, favoured one! The Lord is with you.' ²⁹But she was much perplexed by his words and pondered what sort of greeting this might be. ³⁰The angel said to her, 'Do not be afraid, Mary, for you have found favour with God. ³¹And now, you will conceive in your womb and bear a son, and you will name him Jesus. ³²He will be great, and will be called the Son of the Most High, and the Lord God will give to him the throne of his ancestor David. ³³He will reign over the house of Jacob forever, and of his kingdom there will be no end.' ³⁴Mary said to the angel, 'How can this be, since I am a virgin?' ³⁵The angel said to her, 'The Holy Spirit will come upon you, and the power of the Most High will overshadow you; therefore the child to be born will be holy; he will be called Son of God. ³⁶And now, your relative Elizabeth in her old age has also conceived a son; and this is the sixth month for her who was said to be barren. ³⁷For nothing will be impossible with God.' ³⁸Then Mary said, 'Here am I, the servant of the Lord; let it be with me according to your word.' Then the angel departed from her.

'Can anything good come out of Nazareth?' people said (John 1.46). And yet, in that lost corner of the world, God was preparing the way to renew all humanity. To do this, from the start he asked for the help of simple people: Mary, an unknown girl, to be followed later by shepherds, fishermen . . .

Luke does not conceal Mary's unease when confronted with God's unheard-of promise. But from the beginning of God's covenant with his people, he had begun to prepare this 'yes' in the midst of humanity. He prepared Mary, who is not disbelieving as Sarah was (Gen 18.14), who does not ask for proof like Zechariah (Luke 1.18); she surrenders herself in a transparent 'yes'. She calls herself 'the servant of the Lord': her life will no longer be simply a matter of following her own plans with greater or lesser success. Through it a great mystery will come about: God's visit to human beings.

Her only support for this are in these words: 'Greetings, favoured one! The Lord is with you . . . The child will be called Son of God.' Her trust, even though it will be shared by others (e.g. Luke 1.42; 2.17), will be put to the test by the disconcerting path that Jesus takes. Her struggle will not become any easier as time goes by; it will continue until the cross (John 19.25). After the resurrection, we see Mary praying with the apostles (Acts 1.14). From now on, God will continue to visit human beings through the Church, through each and every believer.

What enables us to keep on saying a 'yes' to God, to take the risk of believing that Christ comes to others through our own life?

How do I express this 'yes' in my daily life?

26
Praise of a heart delivered from fear

LUKE 1.67–79

THEN John's father Zechariah was filled with the Holy Spirit and spoke this prophecy:

[68]'Blessed be the Lord God of Israel,
    for he has looked favourably on his people and redeemed them.
[69]He has raised up a mighty saviour for us
    in the house of his servant David,
[70]as he spoke through the mouth of his holy prophets from of old,
[71]that we would be saved from our enemies and from the hand of all who hate us.
[72]Thus he has shown the mercy promised to our ancestors,
    and has remembered his holy covenant,
[73]the oath that he swore to our ancestor Abraham,
    to grant us [74]that we, being rescued from the hands of our enemies,
might serve him without fear, [75]in holiness and righteousness
    before him all our days.
[76]And you, child, will be called the prophet of the Most High;
    for you will go before the Lord to prepare his ways,
[77]to give knowledge of salvation to his people
    by the forgiveness of their sins.
[78]By the tender mercy of our God,
    the dawn from on high will break upon us,
[79]to give light to those who sit in darkness and in the shadow of death,
    to guide our feet into the way of peace.'

Zechariah did not believe that God could work a miracle in his life (1.5–21). But when he takes the step of believing in God's promise, the hardness of his heart is dissolved, his power of speech returns and a song of praise breaks out. He acclaims the arrival of the moment for which people have been waiting for centuries, the time when 'the rising sun has come to shine on those in darkness and in the shadow of death'. His child John will be John the Baptist, who is to prepare people to receive God himself. Yes, the Great Day has begun; nothing will be able to stop it.

As we sing the Song of Zechariah, we are placed at the heart of this critical moment of human history—the visit of God. Everything changes. The centre of our life shifts. This song turns us toward God so that Christ can flood us with his light. This is the greatest reality that touches our life today.

We need to concentrate no longer on the darkness, both within and around us, but rather to look at reality in the light of the New Covenant: Christ comes to free me from my oppressors and from fear; by his forgiveness he places me, for ever, in the 'tender mercy of our God'; and, still more, God grants me 'to serve him without fear'. When our whole life participates in that radical conversion that makes us see reality in the light of the New Covenant, we ourselves become reflections of God's light. And we find the courage needed to go with Christ even into 'darkness and the shadow of death', to open with him 'a way of peace'.

Have there been times in my life that were like a visit from God?
What is the 'darkness' into which God asks me to go without fear in order to be a peacemaker?

27

Peace on earth

LUKE 2.1–20

I N those days a decree went out from Emperor Augustus that all the world should be registered. [2]This was the first registration and was taken while Quirinius was governor of Syria. [3]All went to their own towns to be registered. [4]Joseph also went from the town of Nazareth in Galilee to Judea, to the city of David called Bethlehem, because he was descended from the house and family of David. [5]He went to be registered with Mary, to whom he was engaged and who was expecting a child. [6]While they were there, the time came for her to deliver her child. [7]And she gave birth to her firstborn son and wrapped him in bands of cloth, and laid him in a manger, because there was no place for them in the inn.

[8]In that region there were shepherds living in the fields, keeping watch over their flock by night. [9]Then an angel of the Lord stood before them, and the glory of the Lord shone around them, and they were terrified. [10]But the angel said to them, 'Do not be afraid; for see—I am bringing you good news of great joy for all the people: [11]to you is born this day in the city of David a Saviour, who is the Messiah, the Lord. [12]This will be a sign for you: you will find a child wrapped in bands of cloth and lying in a manger.' [13]And suddenly there was with the angel a multitude of the heavenly host, praising God and saying,

[14]"Glory to God in the highest heaven,
and on earth peace among those whom he favours!'

[15]When the angels had left them and gone into heaven, the shepherds said to one another, 'Let us go now to Bethlehem and see this thing that has taken place, which the Lord has made known to us.' [16]So they went with haste and found Mary and Joseph, and the child lying in the manger. [17]When they saw this, they made known what had been told them about this child; [18]and all who heard it were amazed at what the shepherds told them. [19]But Mary treasured all these words and pondered them in her heart. [20]The shepherds returned, glorifying and praising God for all they had heard and seen, as it had been told them.

At the centre of the story of Jesus' birth according to St Luke there is the proclamation of peace on earth, made by the angels of God and addressed to human beings, objects of God's saving will. In this way, in Jesus Christ heaven and earth meet; the fullness of a communion unites God and humanity.

For the people of the Bible, peace is the most desired of all realities. The Hebrew word *shalom,* as is well known, is much richer than our word 'peace'; it includes well-being, prosperity, happiness . . . In short, it refers to the fullness of life. A gift of God, peace is at the same time a consequence of the covenant with God, and for this reason the prophets deplore its absence on account of the people's unfaithfulness (Isa 48.18). A longing always remains strong for a new intervention of God who will repair the mistakes of the past and will thus ensure peace for his people, and even for the whole of the human family. People are waiting for a Messiah who will be a 'Prince of Peace' (Isa 9.6), a poor king who will inaugurate the reign of peace 'from sea to sea' (Zech 9.9–10).

This is the longing that, according to Luke, is fulfilled in Jesus. And yet in this story there is suffering (the journey to Bethlehem, the lack of room for the child), poverty (the shepherds were outcasts, despised by all), darkness. If the reign of peace has truly come, it is not as we so often imagine it. Jesus brings peace on earth (cf. 2 Cor 5.17–20; Eph 2.14–18), but not automatically, by magic or by doing violence to human hearts. His presence among human beings is discreet and still it is not without consequences, like the almost invisible yeast that gradually transforms the entire loaf (Matt 13.33).

How does this story help me to understand the manner in which God works in the world to bring us his peace?

How does the image of a tiny baby correspond to God's way of working?

Where is there a need for peace around me? How can we welcome God's peace and bring it to others both near and far?

28
Waiting for the light

LUKE 2.22–40

W HEN the time came for their purification according to the law of Moses, Joseph and Mary brought Jesus up to Jerusalem to present him to the Lord ²³(as it is written in the law of the Lord, 'Every firstborn male shall be designated as holy to the Lord'), ²⁴and they offered a sacrifice according to what is stated in the law of the Lord, 'a pair of turtledoves or two young pigeons'.

²⁵Now there was a man in Jerusalem whose name was Simeon; this man was righteous and devout, looking forward to the consolation of Israel, and the Holy Spirit rested on him. ²⁶It had been revealed to him by the Holy Spirit that he would not see death before he had seen the Lord's Messiah. ²⁷Guided by the Spirit, Simeon came into the temple; and when the parents brought in the child Jesus, to do for him what was customary under the law, ²⁸Simeon took him in his arms and praised God, saying,

> ²⁹"Master, now you are dismissing your servant in peace,
> according to your word;
> ³⁰for my eyes have seen your salvation,
> ³¹ which you have prepared in the presence of all peoples,
> ³²a light for relevation to the Gentiles
> and for glory to your people Israel.'

³³And the child's father and mother were amazed at what was being said about him. ³⁴Then Simeon blessed them and said to his mother Mary, 'This child is destined for the falling and the rising of many in Israel, and to be a sign that will be opposed ³⁵so that the inner thoughts of many will be revealed— and a sword will pierce your own soul too.'

³⁶There was also a prophet, Anna the daughter of Phanuel, of the tribe of Asher. She was of a great age, having lived with her husband seven years after her marriage, ³⁷then as a widow to the age of eighty-four. She never left the temple but worshipped there with fasting and prayer night and day. ³⁸At that moment she came, and began to praise God and to speak about the child to all who were looking for the redemption of Jerusalem.

³⁹When they had finished everything required by the law of the Lord, they returned to Galilee, to their own town of Nazareth. ⁴⁰The child grew and became strong, filled with wisdom; and the favour of God was upon him.

Mary and Joseph take Jesus to the Temple in Jerusalem to be consecrated to God. Christ's whole life is prefigured in this passage: it is in Jerusalem that he will be contradicted, condemned and killed; it is there that he will offer his life; from Jerusalem the light of the Risen Christ will shine out, through the community of the first believers, to the very ends of the earth.

Simeon and Anna are able to discern God's coming in a humble event, as were the shepherds on Christmas night. Simeon recognizes Christ because Simeon bears within himself all the longing of his people which has taken shape in the course of a long history marked by painful events.

The fulfilment of the hope held by only a few prophets has come: in Jesus, God has come for all nations, 'a light for relevation to the Gentiles'. One reason for Christ's being rejected was that he announced God's love for all peoples. What God brings about exceeds the often limited preconceptions of human beings.

What can help us to leave aside all human calculations as we await God's coming into our life?

How can prayer prepare us to recognize the signs of God's presence in our life?

29
Believing in Christ out of love

LUKE 7.36–50

O NE of the Pharisees asked Jesus to eat with him, and he went into the Pharisee's house and took his place at the table. ¹⁷And a woman in the city, who was a sinner, having learned that he was eating in the Pharisee's house, brought an alabaster jar of ointment. ¹⁸She stood behind him at his feet, weeping, and began to bathe his feet with her tears and to dry them with her hair. Then she continued kissing his feet and anointing them with the ointment. ¹⁹Now when the Pharisee who had invited him saw it, he said to himself, 'If this man were a prophet, he would have known who and what kind of woman this is who is touching him—that she is a sinner.' ⁴⁰Jesus spoke up and said to him, 'Simon, I have something to say to you.' 'Teacher,' he replied, 'Speak.' ⁴¹'A certain creditor had two debtors; one owed five hundred denarii, and other fifty. ⁴²When they could not pay, he cancelled the debts for both of them. Now which of them will love him more?' ⁴³Simon answered, 'I suppose the one for whom he cancelled the greater debt.' And Jesus said to him, 'You have judged rightly.' ⁴⁴Then turning toward the woman, he said to Simon, 'Do you see this woman? I entered your house; you gave me no water for my feet, but she has bathed my feet with her tears and dried them with her hair. ⁴⁵You gave me no kiss, but from the time I came in she has not stopped kissing my feet. ⁴⁶You did not anoint my head with oil, but she has anointed my feet with ointment. ⁴⁷Therefore, I tell you, her sins, which were many, have been forgiven; hence she has shown great love. But the one to whom little is forgiven, loves little.' ⁴⁸Then he said to her, 'Your sins are forgiven.' ⁴⁹But those who were at the table with him began to say among themselves, 'Who is this who even forgives sins?' ⁵⁰And he said to the woman, 'Your faith has saved you; go in peace.'

In this Gospel passage, the contrast is not between friends and enemies of Christ. Both persons—Simon, the prominent man, and the woman with a bad reputation—want to be friends with Jesus. Simon invites him for a meal; the woman, unable to do this, comes spontaneously, without being invited, bringing a precious gift.

The conclusion of the story, 'Your faith has saved you', clearly indicates that it deals above all with the road to faith. Why is it that the woman finds the road whereas Simon stops half-way? Simon had certainly invited Jesus with the good intention of knowing him better, of discovering whether he was perhaps the Messiah. If so, he would probably go on to place his trust in him, to believe in him. But he first observes Jesus, without getting involved. He keeps a certain distance ('You gave me no water for my feet', Jesus says to him) to enable him to step back as soon as he judges that Jesus is not the one he is waiting for.

The weeping woman, on the other hand, does not observe Christ nor attempt to form an opinion concerning him. She simply intuits his forgiveness and loves him. And her love for him leads her to faith. It is impossible to grasp the mystery of Christ without loving him with a heart made transparent by his forgiveness. And loving Christ, even without understanding much about him, opens with certainty the road of faith.

What characterizes the attitudes of Simon and the woman toward Jesus? How can we trust and believe in Christ with a loving heart?

30
The light of the Gospel

LUKE 8.16–17

'No one after lighting a lamp hides it under a jar, or puts it under a bed, but puts it on a lampstand, so that those who enter may see the light. ʹFor nothing is hidden that will not be disclosed, nor is anything secret that will not become known and come to light.'

In Jesus' time, the houses of Galilee all had earthenware oil lamps. The task of lighting and putting out one of these lamps was a lot of work, so much so that it was one of the occupations forbidden to perform on the Sabbath! Obviously, it would be absurd to light such a lamp only in order to extinguish it immediately by covering it with a jar (it seems that 'putting a lamp under a jar', a container used for measuring grain or flour, was the usual method of extinguishing a lamp to prevent it from smoking). Though it is theoretically possible, even though ridiculous, to put out a lamp which has just been lit, it is utterly impossible to keep light from illuminating what it shines on. This is what Jesus adds to the parable of the lamp when he says, 'Nothing is hidden that will not be disclosed' (v. 17).

The Gospel of the Kingdom of God is like a lamp which God has lit. Christ is the first bearer of the Good News; he himself is the Gospel. Thus he never let himself be stopped along the way of announcing the Kingdom of God. When people wanted him to stay in Capernaum, the village where he had lived for a while, he answered that he had to move on and announce the Good News elsewhere: that was why he had come (Mark 1.37–38). When he was advised not to go to Jerusalem to bear witness to God, he said, 'I must be on my way' (Luke 13.33). Jesus knew that he was a lamp giving light (he said, 'I am the light of the world' (John 8.12)), and he made the choice not to put out or hide his light.

We too are bearers of the Gospel. Lamps that have been lit. Christ said, 'You are the light of the world' (Matt 5.14). And just as a lamp which does not give light is useless, it is not possible to bear the name of Christ without allowing him to shine through us by the lives we lead. The light of the Gospel, borne by Christ and by Christians, cannot remain hidden.

What does it mean for me, and for my local Christian community, to be a lighted lamp? What does it mean not to put out or hide the light which God has lit in that lamp?

What words of Christ can I receive as a light for my life?

Am I able to make this light visible for others?

31

Without looking back

LUKE 9.57–62

A s they were going along the road, someone said to Jesus, 'I will follow you wherever you go.' [58]And Jesus said to him, 'Foxes have holes, and birds of the air have nests; but the Son of Man has nowhere to lay his head.' [59]To another he said, 'Follow me.' But he said, 'Lord, first let me go and bury my father.' [60]But Jesus said to him, 'Let the dead bury their own dead; but as for you, go and proclaim the kingdom of God.' [61]Another said, 'I will follow you, Lord; but let me first say farewell to those at my home.' [62]Jesus said to him, 'No one who puts a hand to the plough and looks back is fit for the kingdom of God.'

These three rapid dialogues with Christ make us understand, first of all, that following him means entering into dialogue with him. At certain moments in our life, this dialogue takes a precise form. How do Christ's replies come to us?

Jesus invites whoever wants to follow him to remain with him. He has chosen to dwell with us, to such an extent that he no longer has a place to lay his head, no place set apart, protected. Following Jesus, therefore, means entering upon a life in which we are completely linked to his own passionate love for humanity.

In a society where a long time of mourning was the custom, Jesus challenges a disciple to 'let the dead bury their own dead'. This impatience is not a rejection of filial affection, but a reminder of an urgent priority. Proclaiming the Kingdom without delay means discerning, in every situation, the word of life God is addressing to us.

What could be more natural than to look backwards, to want to hold on to what we are leaving, to resist giving everything? And yet Jesus reacts even more strongly in the face of this temptation. To enter fully into the Kingdom of God is possible. And he asks not so much for a heroic act of renunciation, but rather offers to share with us a secret of his life: to receive everything from his Father in the present moment.

Looking at how Christ lived among us, for what other people can I be available with him?

In what way is the proclamation of the Kingdom of God a word of life for me and for people around me?

What have I already learnt to leave behind so as to be ready to welcome what God wants to give me?

32
Loved as the only one

LUKE 19.1–10

J ESUS entered Jericho and was passing through it. ²A man was there named
Zacchaeus; he was a chief tax collector and was rich. ³He was trying to see
who Jesus was, but on account of the crowd he could not, because he was
short in stature. ⁴So he ran ahead and climbed a sycamore tree to see him,
because he was going to pass that way. ⁵When Jesus came to the place, he
looked up and said to him, 'Zacchaeus, hurry and come down; for I must stay
at your house today.' ⁶So he hurried down and was happy to welcome him.
⁷All who saw it began to grumble and said, 'He has gone to be the guest of one
who is a sinner.' ⁸Zacchaeus stood there and said to the Lord, 'Look, half of
my possessions, Lord, I will give to the poor; and if I have defrauded anyone
of anything, I will pay back four times as much.' ⁹Then Jesus said to him,
'Today salvation has come to this house, because he too is a son of Abraham.
¹⁰For the Son of Man came to seek out and to save the lost.'

As a chief tax-collector, Zacchaeus was certainly not loved. Tax-collectors were despised because of their collaboration with the occupying power, and still more because they generally demanded sums greater than those fixed by the official tariffs—which few people would be able to check—and pocketed the surplus. It was said that conversion was ruled out for them for to achieve it they would need to make amends for their wrongdoing and that was impossible—for no human memory, including their own, was capable of counting up the frauds they had committed.

But Christ loved Zacchaeus, the little man perched on his tree. By going to his home, Jesus consciously exposed himself to the loss of his good reputation and to any chance of being listened to in Jericho. Jesus gave all in order to love Zacchaeus. He loved him as if he were the only person who mattered for him, preferring Zacchaeus' house to any other in the city.

Zacchaeus had no time to put things in order or to prepare his house. He understood that in Christ's eyes he counted so much that he was no longer the unloved one but the favourite. Immediately, he responded with joy. And in his celebration with Christ, everything in his life changed.

What did Zacchaeus find in Jesus' attitude to him that made him accept the invitation so quickly and so joyfully?

What touches me the most in Zacchaeus' attitude and actions?

What can tear away the veil of sadness which has been woven by the harsh events of our life and which hides life's beauty?

33
The way of trust

J ESUS said, 'Do not let your hearts be troubled. Believe in God, believe also in me. ²In my Father's house there are many dwelling places. If it were not so, would I have told you that I go to prepare a place for you? ³And if I go and prepare a place for you, I will come again and will take you to myself, so that where I am, there you may be also. ⁴And you know the way to the place where I am going.' ⁵Thomas said to him, 'Lord, we do not know where you are going. How can we know the way?' ⁶Jesus said to him, 'I am the way, and the truth, and the life. No one comes to the Father except through me.'

The Gospel depicts the sombre realism of Thomas the apostle. More quickly than any of the other disciples, he understood the seriousness of the threats hanging over Jesus. In the conspiracies being hatched against Christ, he saw the quickly advancing shadow of death. And so when Jesus announces he is going back to Jerusalem, Thomas, as far-seeing as he is courageous, cries out, 'Let us also go, that we may die with him!' (John 11.16). What path can there be through the realities of death and evil? Thomas sees none (v. 5). And it is not surprising that, after the resurrection, he is the one who needs to see and touch in order to believe (John 20.25).

To believe! This is the verb that is a stumbling-block for Thomas. Jesus uses expressions of great simplicity to invite his disciples to trust. Could he have forgotten the terrible fate awaiting him? The unbearable gap between the anguish of the disciples and Jesus' candour makes Thomas cry out in reproach, 'Lord, we do not know where you are going. How can we know the way?' (v. 5).

A realistic man, Thomas could not discern a way where Jesus was announcing one. He saw only death. Our own questioning, even though it is not directly linked to Jesus' death, is not so very different from Thomas's. We do not want to be naive. As we search for a meaning in life, in the world, in events, we come up against suffering and evil, and we wonder: is there a way through it all? We would like to find an answer to evil, to be able to see and touch that way. Whereas the Gospel asks us first of all to believe. Not in order to make us less realistic, but so that our realism will grow until it can discern, in the concrete situations of the world, with all its suffering, the face of One who is alive.

Can trust help me enter more fully into my own reality?
What supports me in the struggle to believe?

34
Commandment and human creativity

JOHN 15.9–12

' A s the Father has loved me, so I have loved you; abide in my love. [10]If you keep my commandments, you will abide in my love, just as I have kept my Father's commandments and abide in his love. [11]I have said these things to you so that my joy may be in you, and that your joy may be complete.

[12]'This is my commandment, that you love one another as I have loved you.'

The word 'commandment' hurts the ears of many today. It is too suggestive of the military where orders must be followed blindly, with no discussion or reflection. We may be surprised to find it on the lips of Jesus and, still more, to see it linked with love: 'If you keep my commandments, you will abide in my love, just as I have kept my Father's commandments and abide in his love' (v. 10; cf. 14.13–21).

In the Bible, 'commandment' has an original meaning that differs from the simple outward observance of juridical rules. Sometimes, St John uses the term 'word' in places where, in a similar context, he had used 'commandment': 'those who love me will keep my word' (John 14.23). Jesus' commandment is the word he uttered with matchless freedom; it is his entire Gospel, his teaching that astonished all who heard it, opening for them a world whose existence they had never even imagined. We have only to read the Gospel to discover its content: 'This is my commandment, that you love one another as I have loved you' (v. 12). Keeping his commandment means opening ourselves to this love, making it that which gives energy to our daily existences and drawing from it all the resources necessary to translate it into the reality of our lives. From one person to another, from one situation to another—so many possibilities! And so we realize that, if we are to 'keep the commandment', our imagination and intelligence are required and brought into play.

Jesus insists upon this commandment of mutual love; it is his own (v. 12). It will be characteristic of him (John 13.34–35). But when we put it into practice, we do much more than to give life to an institution that is twenty centuries old. Christ—the living Christ and not a memory—remains in those who keep his commandment. In this way, life becomes a creation with him. What better image could we find to describe this mutual and life-giving indwelling than the one used by St John: 'I am the vine, you are the branches. Those who abide in me and I in them bear much fruit' (John 15.5).

In what way is the new commandment of Christ a way of freedom and an invitation to become creators with him?

35

Trust in the Holy Spirit

JOHN 15.26–27

'WHEN the Advocate comes, whom I will send to you from the Father, the Spirit of truth who comes from the Father, he will testify on my behalf. [27]You also are to testify because you have been with me from the beginning.'

As well as believing in Christ, I am asked to believe in his Spirit. If I believe in the Holy Spirit, then I believe in that which the Spirit can accomplish not only in others but also in me. There is no more room then for being pessimistic about myself. Do I know how to love with the selfless love spoken of in the Gospel? Isn't my selfishness too strong? Am I not going to come across it continually, masked in my seemingly best intentions? Trapped by these questions, some people wear themselves out trying to prove to themselves that a new life has begun within them.

Being able to see, feel and experience that the Spirit lives in me is not required of me. What is asked of me is that I believe in the Holy Spirit, that I trust in him, that I abandon myself to him. Far from being yet another demand made on me, this call to faith sets me free. Yes, joyful renunciations do exist. Am I really able to love? I don't know, I accept not knowing and give up my desperate attempts to assure myself of it. I will take seriously the promise of Christ: 'I will not leave you orphaned' (John 14.18).

The Gospel does not forget human limitations. It wants, however, to substitute trust in the Holy Spirit for the worry which they cause. In this way, I can have the courage to be myself. From this moment onwards, I can start to live out the little that I have understood of Christ. My words, clumsy though they may seem, can be used to express my faith. My actions and words will come from me and yet Someone else, without my knowing how, will enable them to be a reflection of Christ. And it is precisely what is best in them that I will probably be unaware of.

How does trust in the Holy Spirit give me the courage to be a witness to Christ and to be myself?

36
Hope will not be disappointed

ROMANS 5.1–8, 10–11

THEREFORE, since we are justified by faith, we have peace with God through our Lord Jesus Christ, ²through whom we have obtained access to this grace in which we stand; and we boast in our hope of sharing the glory of God. ³And not only that, but we also boast in our sufferings, knowing that suffering produces endurance, ⁴and endurance produces character, and character produces hope, ⁵and hope does not disappoint us, because God's love has been poured into our hearts through the Holy Spirit that has been given to us.

⁶For while we were still weak, at the right time Christ died for the ungodly. ⁷Indeed, rarely will anyone die for a righteous person—though perhaps for a good person someone might actually dare to die. ⁸But God proves his love for us in that while we still were sinners Christ died for us. ¹⁰For if while we were enemies, we were reconciled to God through the death of his Son, much more surely, having been reconciled, will we be saved by his life. ¹¹But more than that, we even boast in God through our Lord Jesus Christ, through whom we have now received reconciliation.

Christ puts an end to all judgements which could weigh upon us. For God 'justifies' us; in other words, he removes from our lives everything which goes against his plan of love for us, and gives us our rightful place in a communion with Christ. By trusting alone, we are at peace (v. 2), a peace which is also called reconciliation (v. 11) — the absence of hostility and anguish.

This peace is not passivity; it is dynamic, awaiting at every moment the gift of God. 'We boast in our hope of sharing the glory of God' (v. 2). God's glory had raised Jesus from the dead (Rom 6.4) and, in confident joy, we let God accomplish acts of resurrection in our own lives. In 'sufferings' where there is no way out, during trials when the road seems closed, trust and even joy are possible because God, who gives life to the dead, loves us.

His love is 'poured into our hearts' (v. 5) to fill them to overflowing. Like water which, once it has been poured out, cannot be held back but floods over everything, so God, by the Holy Spirit, gives his love without reserve. What will always characterize this love is that with it God has loved 'his enemies', those who were incapable of responding to him. That is why hope will not disappoint us, because God will never love us less than he did at the moment when he gave everything to us, his forgiveness and his Holy Spirit.

What helps me, instead of withdrawing into myself, to move from fear to peace with God?

How can I look toward God, who raised Christ from the dead, even in situations when there seems to be no way out?

37
Becoming children of God

I F the Spirit of him who raised Jesus from the dead dwells in you, he who raised Christ from the dead will give life to your mortal bodies also through his Spirit that dwells in you.

[12]So then, brothers and sisters, we are debtors, not to the flesh, to live according to the flesh — [13]for if you live according to the flesh, you will die; but if by the Spirit you put to death the deeds of the body, you will live. [14]For all who are led by the Spirit of God are children of God. [15]For you did not receive a spirit of slavery to fall back into fear, but you have received a spirit of adoption. When we cry, 'Abba! Father!' [16]it is that very Spirit bearing witness with our spirit that we are children of God, [17]and if children, then heirs, heirs of God and joint heirs with Christ — if, in fact, we suffer with him so that we may also be glorified with him.

'We are children of God!'—for the first Christians, that was a great discovery (see also 1 John 3.1). The Spirit who raised Jesus from the dead enables us to pray with the word 'Abba', the very same word Jesus used when he spoke to God (Mark 14.36)!

Jesus' entire life was defined by his relationship to the Father (Matt 11.27). Jesus does not want us to see himself alone; he wants us to discover his relationship with God, his Father. That is his secret (Matt 3.17; 17.5): he is the Son; at every moment he receives life from God. Jesus knew that in the events he was called to live God would reveal the fullness of his love. And Christ never lost this confident trust, even in times of temptation and suffering, when events seemed to prove the contrary (John 13.1).

Risen from the dead, Jesus said, 'I am ascending to my Father and your Father' (John 20.17; see also Heb 2.11–13; Eph 2.18). He gave us 'power to become children of God' (John 1.12), people who no longer imagine God as someone arbitrary who would refuse a fullness. Our life is not a more or less fortunate accident; it is entrusted to us by God. And God will not allow that gift to be crushed. Welcoming every moment of our life does not mean becoming fatalists; such an attitude liberates imaginative powers so that we can be creative, even in difficult situations, because it makes more and more room in the depths of our being for a love that chases away fear and bitterness. Christ warned us that this would involve a struggle, because the Tempter does not want us to live in such a trusting relationship with God. But the Holy Spirit constantly reminds us of the truth, so our lips can say the words that Jesus bequeathed to us: 'Our Father . . .'

What helps me to welcome the events of my life and not get lost in dreams of a different world?

Where can we find the courage to go towards those who suffer more than we do, to welcome them and to express our trust that God offers them a hope, that he remains their 'Abba'?

38
Hoping for all

ROMANS 8.18–27

I consider that the sufferings of this present time are not worth comparing with the glory about to be revealed to us. [19]For the creation waits with eager longing for the revealing of the children of God; [20]for the creation was subjected to futility, not of its own will but by the will of the one who subjected it, in hope [21]that the creation itself will be set free from its bondage to decay and will obtain the freedom of the glory of the children of God. [22]We know that the whole creation has been groaning in labour pains until now; [23]and not only the creation, but we ourselves, who have the first fruits of the Spirit, groan inwardly while we wait for adoption, the redemption of our bodies. [24]For in hope we were saved. Now hope that is seen is not hope. For who hopes for what is seen? [25]But if we hope for what we do not see, we wait for it with patience.

[26]Likewise the Spirit helps us in our weakness; for we do not know how to pray as we ought, but that very Spirit intercedes with sighs too deep for words. [27]And God, who searches the heart, knows what is the mind of the Spirit, because the Spirit intercedes for the saints according to the will of God.

In the passage immediately preceding this one, St Paul affirmed that, already at present, we are children of God exactly as Christ is Son of God. We are 'joint heirs with Christ' (v. 17) — everything which belongs to Christ belongs also to us. Why then, in our lives, do we still experience so many trials?

Paul passes without any transition from the trials of Christians to the suffering of 'creation'. (In the language of the milieu from which St Paul comes, this expression generally means all humanity, but here it most likely designates the whole universe — everything created by God.) In their waiting, believers stand alongside the whole human family and all creation. God has imagined one and the same goal for everything that exists: 'the freedom of the glory of the children of God', in other words a kind of existence which, in union with the Risen Lord, has been set free from slavery to fear and resembles God's own existence.

All creation 'is groaning' (v. 22) in labour pains, and Christians too 'grown inwardly while we wait for adoption, the redemption of our bodies' (v. 23), longing for the transfiguration and conforming of our poor bodies to the body of the Risen Christ, as St Paul writes in Philippians 3.21. But the most astonishing thing is that the Holy Spirit too joins in this 'groaning' (v. 26). Waiting, even waiting in pain, is no longer something that happens outside of God. It is God's Spirit who supports us in our waiting and even stimulates this expectant waiting within us. And by the Spirit who intercedes, the groaning of creation and, still more, the groaning of believers is secretly transformed into prayer.

Where around me do I perceive a longing, even a very hidden one, for a communion with the Risen Christ?

What can awaken within us a hope for the whole human family?

How can the mysterious and ceaseless prayer of the Holy Spirit within us set us free from anxiety?

39

One body

F OR just as the body is one and has many members, and all the members of the body, though many, are one body, so it is with Christ. [13]For in the one Spirit we were all baptized into one body—Jews or Greeks, slaves or free—and we were all made to drink of one Spirit.

[14]Indeed, the body does not consist of one member but of many. [15]If the foot would say, 'Because I am not a hand, I do not belong to the body,' that would not make it any less a part of the body. [16]And if the ear would say, 'Because I am not an eye, I do not belong to the body,' that would not make it any less a part of the body. [17]If the whole body were an eye, where would the hearing be? If the whole body were hearing, where would the sense of smell be? [18]But as it is, God arranged the members in the body, each one of them, as he chose. [19]If all were a single member, where would the body be? [20]As it is, there are many members, yet one body. [21]The eye cannot say to the hand, 'I have no need of you,' nor again the head to the feet, 'I have no need of you.' [22]On the contrary, the members of the body that seem to be weaker are indispensable, [23]and those members of the body that we think less honourable we clothe with greater honour, and our less respectable members are treated with greater respect; [24]whereas our more respectable members do not need this. But God has so arranged the body, giving the greater honour to the inferior member, [25]that there may be no dissension within the body, but the members may have the same care for one another. [26]If one member suffers, all suffer together with it; if one member is honoured, all rejoice together with it.

[27]Now you are the body of Christ and individually members of it.

In the New Testament, the call to unity is a priority. This is because with Christ an absolutely new reality has been created: a communion which is not merely the more or less successful juxtaposition of isolated individuals, but a radical dependency on one another. By baptism we have become members of the same body, which constantly receives its life from Christ.

The last evening he spent with his disciples, Jesus prayed that we might be one just as he is one with the Father (John 17.20–24). Christ's love bring us into his own oneness with the Father and creates a communion among us that is a reflection of that unity in the world. This communion is a shared life between Christ and us: 'I am the vine, you are the branches' (John 15.5).

How can we live out this unity in our human relationships? St Paul shows us the way: 'If one member suffers, all suffer together with it. If one member is honoured, all rejoice together with it' (v. 26). Since Christ is in us, I no longer have to be afraid of other persons, to see in them something I do not have, or even to see them as a threat to my own life. I can discover a complementarity between us; still more, I participate in the good that others accomplish; I share in their suffering. Not cutting ourselves off from others in a spirit of comparison, not wishing to affirm ourselves to the detriment of others but trying to be 'in' the other person: this attitude frees us from the need to 'play a role' and makes us joyful at others' gifts. Instead of an individualistic perfection, the Gospel asks us to undertake with our whole being an effort of communion, to let Christ's life circulate. 'Let the same mind be in you that was in Christ Jesus . . .' (Phil 2.5–11).

Who are the people with whom I am called to live a commitment to unity?

How can we express more deeply, in our parishes and communities, that we are one body, dependent upon one another?

40
Finding our identity in a communion

EPHESIANS 4.1–6

I THEREFORE, the prisoner in the Lord, beg you to lead a life worthy of the calling to which you have been called, ²with all humility and gentleness, with patience, bearing with one another in love, ³making every effort to maintain the unity of the Spirit in the bond of peace. ⁴There is one body and one Spirit, just as you were called to the one hope of your calling, ⁵one Lord, one faith, one baptism, ⁶one God and Father of all, who is above all and through all and in all.

All who call themselves Christians live not by themselves
but by a call. Those who bear the name of Christ do not live lives
focused on themselves but on the One who has taken on himself all
that divides, all that separates people from God and from one another.
Living by that call, says the apostle Paul, means 'bearing with one
another in love'.

In the human heart there is a seed of disunion which causes
us often to try and find our own identity by opposition to others.
Sometimes we try to affirm our own worth by holding ourselves apart
from those whose imperfections we discern. Bearing with one another
in love means doing just the opposite: it means, as followers of Christ,
placing ourselves in the other's shoes, and thus bearing the other's
burden. Being weak with other people's weakness, being happy with
their joy—and discovering with astonishment that we find our identity
as unique and irreplaceable persons not by opposition but by
communion.

'There is one Spirit': that becomes the source of a great
peace. Even when oppositions seem to be insurmountable, St Paul
urges those who live by Christ's call to hold fast to the confidence that
the same Spirit of Christ dwells within the hearts of all believers, from
the least to the greatest. And that in the hearts of all, Christ inspires
the same hope for his Church, since he cannot be in contradiction with
himself.

According to this text, what builds up communion?
How can we keep our hearts at peace in the face of harsh opposition?

41
Taken hold of by Christ

I F anyone else has reason to be confident in the flesh, I have more: ⁵circumcised on the eighth day, a member of the people of Israel, of the tribe of Benjamin, a Hebrew born of Hebrews; as to the law, a Pharisee; ⁶as to zeal, a persecutor of the church; as to righteousness under the law, blameless.

⁷Yet whatever gains I had, these I have come to regard as loss because of Christ. ⁸More than that, I regard everything as loss because of the surpassing value of knowing Christ Jesus my Lord. For his sake I have suffered the loss of all things, and I regard them as rubbish, in order that I may gain Christ ⁹and be found in him, not having a righteousness of my own that comes from the law, but one that comes through faith in Christ, the righteousness from God based on faith. ¹⁰I want to know Christ and the power of his resurrection and the sharing of his sufferings by becoming like him in his death, ¹¹if somehow I may attain the resurrection from the dead.

¹²Not that I have already obtained this or have already reached the goal; but I press on to make it my own, because Christ Jesus has made me his own. ¹³Beloved, I do not consider that I have made it my own; but this one thing I do: forgetting what lies behind and straining forward to what lies ahead, ¹⁴I press on toward the goal for the prize of the heavenly call of God in Christ Jesus.

What is the source of our confidence? Where is the foundation of our identity? For the apostle Paul before his encounter with Christ, the response to these questions would have been typical of most of us: a series of acquisitions resulting either from birth or from personal choices. In the course of his life, Paul had constructed an apparently irreproachable personality, worthy of esteem in the eyes of others and (why not?) of God.

But one day, the Risen Christ burst into his life. From then on nothing was the same. His personal qualities appeared to him not only as worthless but even as negative, not because they were bad in themselves but because they had been a barrier between himself and God. They had led him to place his confidence in himself rather than turning to God.

From then on, what mattered most for Paul was a living relationship with Jesus Christ. A relationship in which the paschal mystery, the death and resurrection of Christ, became translated into the concrete circumstances of his life. Rooted in the force of God liberated in the resurrection of Jesus, Paul became able to share the burdens of others and thus participate in the sufferings of Christ. His life became a pilgrimage, or even a race. Christ is both the starting-point and the goal of this race; his simple presence is a call to set out. He frees us from being obsessed with our own situation, from the need to strive for a personal perfection. For the disciple of Christ, the only perfection possible consists in running in his footsteps (cf. Heb 12.1–2), forgetting oneself and one's past, fully open to God in the present moment.

If I had to compose a list such as that in verses 5–6, what would I put in it?

How can we see our personal qualities or accomplishments as gifts of God to be brought to fulfilment rather than as reasons for human glory?

Where does the paschal mystery manifest itself in my life? How do I root myself in the resurrection of Christ? How do I share in his sufferings?

How does the image of the race help me to understand the Gospel?

42

Christ never threatened anyone

1 PETER 2.21–25

F OR to this you have been called, because Christ also suffered for you, leaving you an example, so that you should follow in his steps.

> ²²'He committed no sin,
> and no deceit was found in his mouth.'

²³When he was abused, he did not return abuse; when he suffered, he did not threaten; but he entrusted himself to the one who judges justly. ²⁴He himself bore our sins in his body on the cross, so that, free from sins, we might live for righteousness; by his wounds you have been healed. ²⁵For you were going astray like sheep, but now you have returned to the shepherd and guardian of your souls.

In what way is the passion and death of Jesus a source of life for us? Suffering in itself has no power to liberate, for how could the Lord of life approve of anyone's pain, especially that of his own beloved Son?

In this passage, the apostle Peter reveals the secret to us in these words: 'when he was abused, he did not return abuse; when he suffered, he did not threaten' (v. 23). The passion of Jesus is the site of a mysterious exchange: by responding to human hatred with forgiveness and love, Jesus transformed the torture of the cross into a road to life. If he had fought against his adversaries using the same weapons as they, Jesus would only have caused the spiral of violence to grow greater. Even his own innocence could have become such a weapon, if he had used it as a pretext to justify himself and to exalt himself at others' expense.

By responding to evil with good, Jesus took from evil its power to harm. Evil was overcome by love; in the words of St Paul, 'he put hostility to death' (Eph 2.16). Jesus, the most innocent of all human beings, lived in an authentic solidarity with us, and in this way he did the only thing that could bend human freedom frozen into an attitude of rebellion, of false autonomy. In this way, he put us back on the right path.

What touches me most in the attitude of Christ?

How can we, in the footsteps of Christ, transform the meaning of suffering by the way we deal with it?

43
Becoming like Christ

S EE what love the Father has given us, that we should be called children of
God; and that is what we are. The reason the world does not know us is
that it did not know him. ²Beloved, we are God's children now; what we will
be has not yet been revealed. What we do know is this: when he is revealed, we
will be like him, for we will see him as he is. ³And all who have this hope in
him purify themselves, just as he is pure.

One day or another, every human being asks themselves
the question 'Who am I?' Knowing oneself is one of the deepest
aspirations of the human heart. And since faith never takes us out of
the human condition, believers are not exempt from such questioning.
But what is dangerous in this search for one's own identity are answers
that imprison us and keep us from growing, answers that inhibit a
possible transfiguration of what we are.

In order to know ourselves, St John invites us to turn our
eyes toward God. He is aware of the difficulty many Christians have in
discovering the beauty of their lives because those around them
constantly misunderstand what they are all about. He writes: 'The
world does not know us.' And since we are all sensitive to the opinions
others have of us, our self-esteem is necessarily affected when we are
misunderstood, when our intentions are distorted.

Fixing our eyes on the love God gives us in his constant
presence and forgiveness, is what helps us to understand who we are:
God's beloved children, in the very same way that Christ is God's
beloved Son.

But what can we do when the disparity between what we
know from Christ and what we discover in our own lives seems
insurmountable? There is only one way that brings us into a unity of
life with Christ. That road consists in trusting that we are already
what we shall one day be, even though it is not yet visible. There is
nothing we can do to make ourselves like Christ. But whoever
concentrates on the love God has for them and believes that that is
what they already are, becomes it for sure (in verse 3,'hope' does not
mean 'uncertainty', but rather confidence turned toward the future).

*What helps me not to become paralysed by judgements or criticisms that
others make about me (or that I make about myself)?*

*What enables us to live in the confidence that, in a hidden way, we already are
what we shall one day be in the light of Christ?*

44
The voice of the Beloved

REVELATION 3.20

'LISTEN! I am standing at the door, knocking; if you hear my voice and open the door, I will come in to you and eat with you, and you with me.'

The Risen Christ sums up the Gospel message in some simple but fundamental words. From the beginning, God has been looking for human beings in order to enter into a relationship with us. At the same time, God never imposes himself or forces us to respond. And through Christ, God knocks, like a poor man, at the door of every human heart.

In the Bible, eating together is a sign of fellowship or communion, of a shared life. This communion becomes a reality for those who open their door to Christ (cf. John 14.23). Our faith does not require us to do great things, but simply to discern God's call and to respond by a movement of welcome, of inner openness. And this simple act is, in fact, everything: like the response of Mary (Luke 1.26–38), it enables God to enter the world through our own existence.

In the midst of the noises of the world, how can we discern the voice of Christ who stands at our door?

How can we open our door to Christ?

What concrete steps or attitudes towards others follow from this inner movement by which we welcome Christ?

THE TAIZÉ COMMUNITY

'A Parable of Communion'
August 1940, with Europe in the grip of World War II, Brother Roger, aged 25, set up home in the almost abandoned village of Taizé, in eastern France. His dream: to bring together a monastic community which would live out 'a parable of community', a parable to be set at the heart of the distress of the time. Centring his life on prayer, he used his house to conceal refugees, especially Jews fleeing from the Nazi occupation.

An International Ecumenical Community
Taizé's founder spent the first two years alone. Others joined him later and at Easter 1949, seven brothers commited themselves together in the common life and celibacy. Year by year, still others have entered the community, each one making a lifelong commitment after several years of preparation. Today, there are 90 brothers, Catholics and from various Protestant backgrounds, from over twenty different countries. Some of them are living in small 'fraternities' in poor neighbourhoods in Asia, Africa, North and South America. The brothers accept no donations or gifts for themselves, not even family inheritances, and the community holds no capital. The brothers earn their living and share with others entirely through their own work.

In 1966, Sisters of Saint Andrew, an international Catholic community founded 750 years ago, came to live in the neighbouring village, to share the responsibility of welcoming people in Taizé.

Taizé and the Young: The Intercontinental Meetings
Young people, and less young, have been coming to Taizé in ever greater numbers since 1957. Hundreds of thousands of people from Europe and far beyond have thus been brought together in a common search. Intercontinental meetings take place each week, Sunday to Sunday, throughout the year and they include youth from between 35 and 60 countries during any one week. The meetings give each person an opportunity to explore the well-springs of faith and to reflect on how to unite the inner life and human solidarity. The meetings in summer can have up to 6,000 participants a week. The greatest numbers gather at Easter, Pentecost and All Saints. Three times every day, the brothers and everybody on the hill come together for common prayer in the Church of Reconciliation, built in 1962 when the church in the village became too small.

'The Pilgrimage of Trust on Earth'
The community has never wanted to create a 'movement' around itself and young people are called rather to commit themselves in their church at home, in their neighbourhood, their city or village, or in their parish. To support them in this, Taizé is animating 'a pilgrimage of trust on earth'. At the end of each year, a major gathering, bringing together tens of thousands of young adults for several days, takes place in a city of Eastern or Western Europe. The most recent of these saw 75,000 young adults together in Budapest, Hungary. From time to time similar meetings are held on other continents also. Madras, India, has hosted two; in February 1991, Manila in the Philippines welcomed young people from all parts of Asia and beyond; and a North American gathering is planned for May 1992.

TO FIND OUT MORE ABOUT TAIZÉ

The Taizé Experience
A book of photographs by Vladimir Sichov with texts by Brother Roger
Geoffrey Chapman Mowbray, Stanley House, Fleets Lane, Poole BH15 3AJ, UK; The
Liturgical Press, St John's Abbey, Collegeville, MN 56321, USA

The Story of Taizé
From the beginnings to the present-day intercontinental meetings
By J. L. González Balado
Geoffrey Chapman Mowbray; The Liturgical Press

A Pilgrimage of Trust on Earth
Booklet of colour photographs with texts on the community and the meetings
Geoffrey Chapman Mowbray

Taizé — Trust is at Hand   28-minute VHS PAL video cassette
The community and the intercontinental meetings in Taizé and outside of
Taizé, in Eastern Europe, India, the Philippines, Paris, Brother Roger at
UNESCO, etc.
Geoffrey Chapman Mowbray; Rainbow Book Agencies, 134 Emmaline Street, PO Box
58, Northcote, Vic 3070, Australia
American version in VHS NTSC: Credence Cassettes, 115 East Armour Boulevard, Box
414291, Kansas City, MO 64141–4291, USA

Europe: Awakened from Within   24-minute VHS PAL video cassette
A Taizé European Meeting, like the one which brought together 50,000 young
people from East and West in Wrocław, Poland, provides a very special
view of the European family.
Ateliers et Presses de Taizé, 71250 Taizé Community, France

Seeds of Trust   28-minute VHS PAL and NT8C video cassette
The 1990 European Meeting in Prague, the 1991 Asian Meeting in Manila
and the Easter celebrations in Taizé show how Taizé's vocation is the same
everywhere.
Ateliers et Presses de Taizé

✻   ✻   ✻

No Greater Love: Sources of Taizé by Brother Roger of Taizé
*'This short book contains what is perhaps the secret of this extraordinary
adventure of faith.'*
Geoffrey Chapman Mowbray; The Liturgical Press

His Love is a Fire by Brother Roger of Taizé
Central writings with extracts from journals
Geoffrey Chapman Mowbray; St Paul Publications, 60–70 Broughton Road, Homebush,
NSW 2140, Australia; The Liturgical Press

Meditations on the Way of the Cross
by Mother Teresa of Calcutta and Brother Roger of Taizé
Geoffrey Chapman Mowbray; The Pilgrim Press, 132 West 31 Street, New York, NY
10001, USA

Mary Mother of Reconciliations
by Mother Teresa of Calcutta and Brother Roger of Taizé
Geoffrey Chapman Mowbray; St Paul Publications; Paulist Press, 997 Macarthur Boulevard, Mahwah, NJ 07430, USA

Life from Within
Prayers by Brother Roger and icons from the Church of Reconciliation
Geoffrey Chapman Mowbray; W/JKP, 100 Witherspoon Street, Louisville, KY 40202-1396, USA

                            *   *   *

Songs and Prayers from Taizé   80-page booklet
Suggestions for preparing prayers in groups and parishes and 50 songs from Taizé, each with musical setting, in its original language and an English-language version
Geoffrey Chapman Mowbray; Rainbow Book Agencies; GIA Publications, 7404 South Mason Avenue, Chicago, IL 60630, USA

Songs and Prayers from Taizé   Music cassette
Presenting twenty songs from the booklet. Recorded in St Paul's Church, Clifton, Bristol, UK in May 1991.
Geoffrey Chapman Mowbray; Rainbow Book Agencies; GIA Publications

Other music cassettes:

Canons et Litanies—Cantate (also on CD)
Alleluia (also on CD)—**Resurrexit** (also on CD)
Jubilate (also on CD)
Distribution: Redemptorist Publications, Alphonsus House, Chawton, Alton GU3 3HQ, UK; Rainbow Book Agencies; GIA Publications

Music from Taizé   Two volumes. Vocal and instrumental editions.

HarperCollins, Westerhill Road, Bishopbriggs, Glasgow G64 2QT, UK; Collins Dove, PO Box 316 Blackburn, Vic 3130, Australia; GIA Publications
Geoffrey Chapman Mowbray books are distributed in Australia by Charles Paine Pty Ltd, 8 Ferris Street, 1 North Parramatta, NSW 2151

The Letter from Taizé
Every two months, in fifteen languages, news of the pilgrimage of trust from across the world, themes for group reflection, texts for meditation, prayers and daily Bible readings. Subscriptions: write to Taizé.

Address: The Taizé Community, 71250 Cluny, France
Telephone: Community (33) 85.50.30.30. Meetings (33) 85.50.30.02
Fax: (33) 85.50.30.15   *Telex*: 800753 COTAIZÉ